UPON THE FACE OF THE WATERS

Ruthie M. Counter

GROW+BLESS BOOKS

Cover design by Rob Barge, Hardware Graphic Design

UPON THE FACE OF THE WATERS
Copyright © 2023 by Ruthie M. Counter
Published by Grow+Bless Books LLC
Champaign, Illinois 61821
rmcounter.wixsite.com/growandbless

Publisher's Cataloging-in-Publication data
Names: Counter, Ruthie M., author.
Title: Upon the face of the waters : sensing the spirit's presence in troubling times / Ruthie M. Counter
Description: Includes bibliographical references. | Champaign, IL: Grow+Bless Books LLC, 2023.
Identifiers: LCCN: 2023906962 | ISBN 979-8-9880437-0-6 (paperback) | 979-8-9880437-1-3 (ebook)
Subjects: LCSH Christian women--Religious life. | Women--Religious aspects--Christianity. | Consolation. | Spiritual life--Christianity. | Christian life. | BISAC RELIGION / Christian Living / Women's Interests
Classification: LCC BV4527 .C68 2023 | DDC 248.8/43--dc23

Printed in the United States of America

For my mother,

who led me to Christ by her Spirit-infused example of faith.

Acknowledgments

I would like to thank:

- God's Holy Spirit for tenderly hovering over me, helping me at this very moment. There would be no book without You.

- all the ladies whom I asked to contribute a story, and especially to those who accepted the challenge and provided Spirit-filled testimony, for sharing their lives with us, revealing snapshots of troubling times covered by God's grace. We are all the better for your having done so.

- my patient, godly editor, Cynthia McEntire, for letting the Spirit use her blessed skills to augment the clarity and flow of this book at its initial review. I am grateful for you.

- my sisters, both natural and spiritual, who reviewed excerpts of this book, for continually checking on its progress and tenderly encouraging me to complete it.

- my writing coach, author Cindi McMenamin, for guiding me from incomplete manuscript to publication. God's Spirit hovered over our sessions, leading to what I pray will be a blessing to many.

Finally, I thank you, dear reader who desires closeness with God, for taking time to reflect on His Word and on His Spirit's active, caring, and effective presence in your life during tough times. May He move you even nearer to Himself through these pages.

CONTENTS

Troubles, Transformations, and Big Reveals

Whether you turn to the right or to the left, your ears will hear a voice behind you, saying, "This is the way; walk in it."
ISAIAH 30:21

I remember my mother standing at our kitchen sink, on the west end of the small two-bedroom house I shared with my parents and six siblings. She faced the wall, her head slightly lowered, washing dinner dishes. Standing a few feet behind her at an angle, I couldn't fully see her expression. Still, her heart was so heavy, I could almost feel her pain without seeing her face.

Moments earlier, her husband (my father), had come through the back door of our house and into the kitchen to begin one of his roaring, drunken rages. Again. As Momma continued washing dishes, she looked up at a white business envelope taped to the wall in front of her. (She often wrote out budgets and notes for herself on the envelopes of bills that came in the mail.) On one side of this envelope, in her handwriting, was a single scripture, Psalm 121:1-2, which nearly spanned the length of the envelope:

> I will lift up mine eyes unto the hills, from whence
> cometh my help. My help cometh from the LORD,
> the maker of heaven and earth (KJV).

Then, out of her deep valley of sadness, surrounded by the anger-filled echoes of the one she loved most on earth, Momma quietly began to sing. It was a soft, low moan of praise to God, an airing of Christ's reign over her life. In one of her favorite hymns, she declared the Lord's mercies and recognized that He was blessing her, even in that awful, trouble-filled moment, even though she might not have been able to see what it was He was doing for her.

Like a bullet to my seven-year-old heart, Momma's song filled my ears and filled the kitchen and the house and seemed to fill even the modest Gary, Indiana, neighborhood where we lived. Every once in a while, a song or one of the scriptures she softly recited would fill Daddy's ears, too, and begin reproaching his heart. But he quickly would shake it off, pick up his complaints, and hurl them at her back once again.

How sad and lonely Momma felt during those abusive moments. How did she maintain such composure in the dark valley? How did she not only resist arguing, complaining, or even imploring my dad to stop his verbal assault, but instead focused on God's Word and sang praises?

I believe she was able to do this because, although she felt lonely, she recognized that she was not alone in the trial she was facing. She trusted that her Lord, the Maker of Heaven and Earth, was there to help her. I believe God's Holy Spirit was there, tenderly hovering over Momma in that moment at that kitchen sink in Gary. I didn't recognize His presence, not at the time. But He was there, doing what He does best: guiding her responses, comforting her heart with the Word, and encouraging her toward prayer and praise.

Now before I reveal to you what He saw there at that sink that none of us could see, let me share a little more with you about this helping, hovering Holy Spirit.

God's Hovering Holy Spirit

According to Genesis 1:2, the Holy Spirit, one of the Three Persons of Elohim (God), makes His silent appearance at the very dawn of time:

> And the earth was without form, and void; and darkness
> was upon the face of the deep. And the Spirit of God
> moved upon the face of the waters (KJV).

Did you ever notice that God's Spirit was *moving* over the formless void that was Earth? Take a moment to picture it: Despite the vast, dark emptiness, the Spirit was hovering just above it in anticipation, at just the right vantage point to witness any activity that would take place.

And what happened as the Spirit moved over the Big Void? Only the most amazingly creative transformation that has ever taken place. Or ever will. It was Earth's big reveal.

Light where there was no sun. Water held afloat by invisible gasses thousands of feet above sea level. Land forming where only water had stood. A bounty of lush green grasses, plants, and vibrant fruit trees, all kept fresh and growing without a drop of rain. Later, a sun to control the weather, with a smaller moon hanging nearby reflecting the sun's light and helping with night vision, time determination, and weather.

God the Father had thought of absolutely everything: an immense variety of sea, air, and land animals, some of which still have not been discovered. Brachiosauruses reaching 75 feet and giant Sequoias spanning four times their height, nearly the length of a football field. Tiny copepods feeding enormous blue whales. The spectacular colors and breathtaking biodiversity, along with the beauty, majesty, delicacy, and savage fierceness of the wild beings, would all prove God to be, not just a creator, but THE Creator. What God the Father spoke, God the Son brought into existence and held (and still holds) together (Colossians 1:16-17; John 1:1-3). Being God, too, the Holy Spirit knew this transformation was about to happen but must have been very impressed with the outcome nonetheless (Genesis 1:31).

Throughout the Bible, this same Holy Spirit hovered over and interacted with men and women, from Israel's patriarchs, judges, and kings to God's prophets and Christ's apostles. He transformed their personalities, guided their paths, and encouraged prayer and praise. He also gave gifts and brought strength and comfort during persecutions and other troubles. (For examples, see Judges 14:6 and 11:29; 1 Samuel 10:5-6; Psalm 5:10-12; 1 Corinthians 12:4, 7-11; Ephesians 6:18; and Jude 20).

Here's some good news: This very same Holy Spirit still hovers over you and me today, and He desires to interact with us in the same ways. He speaks to us and teaches us, grieves when we sin, and guides us step by step through life's difficulties if we're willing to keep in step with Him (Revelation 3:22; John 14:26; Ephesians 4:30; Galatians 5:25). He even prays for us in our weaknesses, interpreting our anguished prayers to God through groanings too deep for words (Romans 8:26). Can you sense His tender presence upon you, hovering over each trial you face in every role you carry as a woman?

Our Helper in Trouble for Every Role

As women, you and I can take on multiple life roles at any given moment. Some of us wear our titles proudly, like wife, mother, Christian, or servant. Some of us carry titles we didn't necessarily choose, like daughter, sister, or student. Whether we choose them or they choose us, all the roles we fulfill in life come with their own share of joys and sorrows, hills and valleys, and none of us are immune from experiencing an anxiety-inducing or angst-filled time or two as we're holding one or more of these roles.

But whatever your troubling time or difficulty, whatever loneliness, sickness, loss, lack, fear, or conflict you may be enduring, you should know that the very real presence of God's Holy Spirit is near you as you go through it. The Spirit has been given an even more active role in the daily lives of Christians, guiding us in God's truth (John 16:13; 15:26) to bring us inexplicable peace. So, acknowledging His nearness to you and letting Him guide you in doing God's will can mean all the difference in the outcome of your troubles, no matter your role.

That's what this book, with its biblical and present-day stories of women facing trouble, is all about. Each story you read here is meant to stand alone. Each of these women, with her trials and triumphs, carries a powerful, self-containing lesson. Some of these stories are dramatized versions of what certain women from the Bible endured in the face of troubling times. Other stories offer firsthand accounts from Christian women I know and admire, shared through their own words.

And what troubles these women faced: Marriages in turmoil, infertility, devastating diagnoses, the crushing sorrow of loss, abuse. They cried, prepared, prayed, and praised God through the dark voids. Yet these women became overcomers through their trust in God and through guidance from His Spirit of power!

The One Who Sees Our Big Reveals

In some of these stories, the Holy Spirit's movement over a woman's life led to what I like to call her *big reveal*—an outcome which showed that her troubles had been no match for God's transformative power. In her big reveal, it's clear that her difficulties did not represent the meaning of her life or dictate His final purpose for her.

Just like at Earth's transformation, the full beauty of these big reveals may have taken a while to arrive, but the hovering Spirit witnessed them all and likely was, as I am today, impressed with the Son's work in shaping these women's lives. And why not be impressed? Scripture tells us He who began a good work in us is still carrying on that work to completion until the Day He comes back for us (Philippians 1:6).

My mother's own big reveal turned out to be a lovely one for the Spirit to witness as well.

Momma's (and Daddy's) Big Reveal

Years after that troubling moment in our kitchen, my father chose not only to put away his alcohol abuse for good, but to recommit his life to love, worship, and serve Jesus Christ. That's right. Daddy became one of the leading servants in the church my mother attended, giving communion talks and becoming a spiritual mentor, a caretaker of facility and grounds, and a Sunday school director. (The prayers of righteous women and men availed much on his behalf.) I felt so proud of his progress in the Lord.

What's more, as the Son transformed my father, He also transformed my mother. As Momma renewed her mind daily in God's Word (Romans 12:2), He built in her an indomitable faith and perseverance that endured decades of difficult moments as she still diligently cared for her husband's needs and managed her household, in true Proverbs 31-woman style.

Funny thing about transformations, though: They don't happen overnight. In fact, Daddy would drink and rage for another seven years after that moment in the kitchen, something he had been doing for probably a decade prior to that point. Nonetheless, the Spirit was moving over their lives, comforting, guiding, and watching Christ work. Remember, while the final, full *result* of a transformation—those big changes you observe and praise God for—seems to arise suddenly out of nowhere, the *process* of transformation—those subtle yet forward-moving changes you don't detect—happen constantly under the watchful eye of the Holy Spirit.

And just as the latter half of Job's troubled life was peace-filled and blessed (Job 42:12-16), so were my mom's and dad's lives. They were married 67 years before my dad's death in January 2020, and he had been sober for the latter 40. During that time, they celebrated anniversaries surrounded by children and grandchildren, took cruises and romantic trips together, served God together, and even dressed in same-colored suits on Sunday mornings (Daddy's idea). They watched their descendants earn degrees and travel the world.

Yes, even through all that prior tumbling through the void of rough, dark waters, my parents' lives were progressing toward a bright, useful, and God-honoring future together. And who saw all that change occurring before the big reveal? The Holy Spirit.

My parents' story is not unique. The Holy Spirit of Almighty Yahweh moves over your troubled waters, too, even today. But don't go ahead of Jesus and try to fix things yourself. Be still, praying and obeying the Spirit's faithful guidance, and wait on The Creator to act powerfully on your behalf (Psalm 27:14; 37:7). Your big reveal is sure to be awesome.

How to Use This Book

As you read in this book the stories of real women facing troubles, my prayer is that you become convinced that God's Holy Spirit plays an active role in your life today:

- comforting you within your troubled waters;
- encouraging you to pray, praise, and obey God;
- interceding for you;
- and tenderly guiding you day by day toward your big reveal.

May you come away from these scenarios understanding that no matter how dark and scary the void you find yourself facing, your own story is far from finished and especially, that you're not facing the void alone. I pray their stories help you gain greater confidence that God is with you and will help you through your challenging times, great or small. And I hope you come to sense His Spirit's tender, guiding movement in the midst of it all.

Suggestions for Chapter Reading

While it is fine to read this book straight through in chapter order, you may find it more useful to begin with a look at the Contents page to see if a topic catches your eye. Alternatively, you could first consider which of your life roles is currently presenting you with the greatest challenge, and then start your reading journey from that section. Wherever you decide to start, let me encourage you to pray beforehand that God will make it clear where you should begin.

Next, no matter what stage of life you find yourself in at the moment, carve out a little time for yourself to absorb what you're reading in these pages. If you can only find five minutes alone in a quiet space, then read just a few pages at a time. I encourage you to not be in a hurry as you digest and understand the details God has given us about His Spirit's tender workings in our lives, even if you must take it in one spoonful at a time.

Here's one way to use those five minutes effectively: As you begin each new chapter, be sure to read that chapter's featured Bible scripture before exploring any of the accompanying story text. The power for positive life change lies in God's Holy Word, not in any woman's experience of God, no matter how inspirational that experience may be. Again, please remember to pray for insight before each reading.

Perhaps life presently allows you more extensive time to read full chapters in one sitting. If so, and you desire to explore God's message to you even further, I invite you to also pause and consider the reflection and application questions that follow each chapter. Read the Bible references. I've left space after each question or suggested application so you can write down your thoughts as a way of engaging with this material and remembering your answers or applications so they don't slip away after you've closed the book.

Are you currently part of a book club, or are you able to study with friends? If so, I hope the group questions in the Food for Thought section (at the back of the book) will prove beneficial to you. All of these questions expand on the concept of the Spirit's movement in your troubles and challenges, with additional Bible references and suggestions for your personal practice in godliness.

Further Study on the Spirit

Speaking of more extensive exploration, let me ask you: Will reading this book provide you with everything you need to know about how the Holy Spirit acts during your troubled times? By no means! This work barely scratches the surface in explaining the Spirit's involvement and work in your life. However, it may prove to be a launching pad into this fascinating subject. A more in-depth, personal study of God's Word will offer you greater insight into the promised Holy Spirit, whom you receive through faith (Galatians 3:14). I invite you to dig deeper.

Assurance the Spirit Lives in You

Finally, if you believe in God but aren't sure you have the indwelling Spirit of God in your life, let's be sure of that right now. Go to the section titled, "Unwrap the Gift of the Spirit," on page 161 and read how you can know for sure that you are a child of God, forgiven and set free through Christ, and indwelt by His Holy Spirit. For His Spirit doesn't only hover over our lives, watching us; He guides us by living in our hearts.

And if you know for sure that you have God's Spirit living in you, having repented of your sins and surrendered your life to Christ, I feel blessed and honored that you are here with me to explore how the Holy Spirit helps you through troubles as you read these women's stories. Of course, you already understand that yours is the Best Story of All: You are forgiven! You have been rescued by His Son, Jesus, the Prince of Peace. He delivered up His sinless human body—His perfect life—so you could live with Him and His Father in joy-filled peace forever. They're expecting to receive you in a beautiful eternal home, prepared just for you.

This book is merely an opportunity for you to discover how God's hovering Holy Spirit gently escorts you up to your new front door.

PART I

HOVERING OVER YOU – THE FRIEND OF JESUS

Friend of Jesus" is likely not a title you would use to describe yourself, is it? "Mom," "wife," or "businesswoman," sure, but "friend of Jesus?" Yes! I believe "friend of Jesus" is the most important title you can wear. Because you are Jesus' friend, your joy will be complete, your hope, secure (John 15:15, 11).

Many faithful women served as friends of Jesus during His earthly ministry (Luke 8:1-3). They traveled with Him, paid for food and supplies and, like His friend Martha, invited others into their homes to hear Him teach. These women friends of Jesus stood near Him as He was being crucified, treading where most of His male disciples would not dare go. In return, Jesus loved them: He called them by name, healed their diseases, instructed them, and elevated the status of women in His day. He was *their* friend, too.

Did you know that, as you live your life as a modern-day friend of Jesus, you can receive the same intimate grace from Him that these women of old received? *You can.* He hears your cries for personal healing and calls you by name, just like His friend, college professor Kendra McClure, will show you in chapter two. He puts His Spirit in your heart as a deposit, instructing you and guaranteeing your elevated status with Him in heavenly places (2 Corinthians 1:22; Ephesians 1:14). Most importantly, He promises *never* to leave you nor forsake you (Hebrews 13:5-6). Now that's a true friend.

Let the following stories show you how the Holy Spirit gently delivers out-of-this-world comfort to you as a friend of Jesus facing major life troubles (Philippians 4:7).

1

MARTHA: BUT EVEN NOW

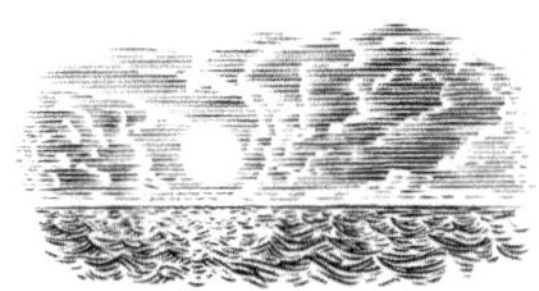

"But I know that even now God will give you whatever you ask."
JOHN 11:22

Martha had waited for Jesus to come, to help them. But when He arrived, it was too late to help. Her brother Lazarus had died.

In fact, it had been four days now since Lazarus had died, and those days had been a whirlwind. There were burial arrangements to make, her sister Mary to console, grieving friends and family to feed. Oh, so many friends and family! Martha was glad many of them had brought food along with them to help feed the hungry mourners who came and went.

Because it fell in her lap to ensure that Lazarus' final affairs were handled properly, Martha had little time to dress the gaping wound of grief she carried around in her own heart. It had been enough for her to manage the load for the family, heavy though it was. Still, she had never felt more alone: alone in those sad days of sickness and death before Lazarus died, alone in her sorrow at his passing, alone even though she was surrounded by well-meaning friends and family members. Yet, Martha wasn't alone.

The Holy Spirit was hovering over the dark void of grief into which Martha's heart had fallen. He had long hovered over her household, instilling hope and trust in the Messiah, because He knew this trial was coming. But being infinite and unhindered by time, the Spirit also could see that Martha's Friend and Master, the Lord Jesus, was not only going to arrive right on time but was going to shine His bright light directly into her void. The Spirit was about to witness Martha's big reveal.

Martha the Trusting

Now that Jesus had arrived, Martha did begin to feel a little less alone. After all, she loved her Lord and knew He loved her. She believed that, had He come just four days earlier, He would have been able to heal His cherished friend Lazarus of his fatal disease. She had witnessed Jesus heal so many other people. Yet she also understood that He had an insanely busy ministry to fulfill. Despite her painful circumstances, Martha wanted to reassure Jesus of her continued friendship, loyalty, and trust in His power. So, before He and His disciples could fully enter town, Martha went out to meet Him and when she did so, she made an extraordinary declaration of faith: "But I know that even now God will give you whatever you ask," she told Him.

"Even now, God will give." Even now, Jesus, if You wanted to miraculously heal someone else, Your Father would do it for You in a heartbeat. Even now. I believe.

Martha the Beloved

I'm encouraged that Martha heads the list of godly women featured in these pages. For far too long, Martha has been studied more for her failings than her faith, known more for her humbling by Jesus than for her having very human reactions to stressors. But John, the beloved disciple of Jesus and the writer of this account, tells us plainly that "Jesus loved Martha" (John 11:5), even mentioning her by name in Jesus' affection *before* her siblings! And John certainly would have recognized Jesus' family-like affection toward someone, for John had held this same close, familial bond with Jesus himself (John 13:23).

Like Jesus, I love Martha. I love how relatable she is. I love her willingness to express her feelings, right or wrong, to her friend, the

Rabbi. I love how she allowed Him to mold her in honest, hands-on fashion, like a potter molds misshapen clay. When refined in the kiln of troublesome times, such human clay can produce the strongest and most useful vessels for God.

Of course, sometimes the Potter's molding discipline can sting. Martha knew this. Jesus once chided her, "Martha, Martha…you are worried and upset about many things," yet God is all you need (Luke 10:41-42). Ah, how she knew He had been so right; how He could see right through her! He could sense her anxiety in ensuring that everyone had everything they needed while in her house. *Will I have enough food to feed everyone adequately, once the Lord has concluded His talk?* she remembered thinking. *Will everything taste okay?* She realized even then that, although she trusted Jesus, He still had much to teach her about quiet trust.

The Rabbi read my inner thoughts as though I had said them aloud, she must have remembered. *So I know that whatever He asks God for, He will receive it. Even now.*

When Grief Must Be His Will

After hearing Martha's stellar declaration of faith in Him, Jesus gave her the news she surely had been longing to hear: "Lazarus will rise again." Well, even in her grief, Martha believed this. She had reasoned that, although Lazarus couldn't be with her any longer, surely she would be with him again one day, resurrected with him on that Last Day her Lord often spoke about.

Martha figured that Jesus, her Lord and friend, had now come to town to remind her of this resurrection, to comfort her and her sister Mary in their present grief. After all, He had not come in time to keep Lazarus from dying, so it must have been His will for Lazarus to die.

Wait…what?

You know, we can have thoughts and make assumptions like this when our troubles seem great or endless, can't we? If God delays in delivering us from what ails, grieves, or torments us, we can begin to reason that it's really too late for Him to turn things around on our behalf. Even though we still believe He performs miracles for others, we resolve that it must be in His will for us to suffer our woes.

Of course, the Lord did warn us that we would have trouble in this world (John 16:33). But what if, instead of watching us resign to our troubles, figuring that His delay in acting has made rescue or relief impossible, Jesus is waiting for us to believe the impossible could happen *even now*–for *us*–when all hope seems lost? What if He wants us to throw out a last-minute, "Hail Mary" pass of faith?

Was Martha making such a pass earlier, with her "but even now" declaration? Perhaps. In fact, I think the idea of Jesus' raising Lazarus from the grave wasn't a stretch for Martha to believe. However, a couple of problem questions might have choked her Hail Mary pass: 1) Did Jesus even want to bring Lazarus back from the dead? 2) How exactly would He go about performing such a miracle?

Problem Question #1: Does God Want to Rescue?

This first problem question goes along with the earlier notion that it is "too late" to be rescued from our trials. Sometimes, we figure we're not all that worthy of saving, anyway, that God must be sick of us and so has turned away or no longer cares to help. Sometimes we think this way because we've made some grave mistakes in the past, or we're in some habitual sin we can't seem to overcome, or we have hurt others in ways we feel are too heinous for God to fully forgive. Why would He want to rescue those who don't deserve rescue?

The truth is, God desires to help us in our life troubles despite our sinful past. Think of Zacchaeus, the woman caught in adultery, the Samaritan woman with her five ex-husbands and live-in lover, or the thief on the cross. Remember David, Moses, and Paul. Although these people committed willful, selfish, habitual, or hurtful sins, even crimes, God found them worthy of rescue. He reached out to them first, acknowledging their sins but willingly offering pardon and newness of life. As each sinner was willing to grab hold of His lifeline and make that Hail Mary pass of faith in His love, their life was irrevocably blessed.

Won't you choose to believe, like they did, that He actually does want to rescue someone like you, even now?

Problem Question # 2: How Will Rescue Happen?

Martha may have been a believer, but she was also a realist. The realistic side of her psyche clashed with the notion of last-minute recovery for Lazarus. Her thoughts must have raced as Jesus approached Lazarus' tomb and began commanding men nearby to roll away the stone that sealed it: *Wait, do you intend to expose his stinking, decayed flesh to the public? Is that really necessary to rescue my brother, Jesus? Must you roll away the stone to revive the dead?*

Martha's embarrassment about exposing the stench of human decay reminds me of you and me. Sure, we want God to forgive us and rescue us from trouble, but we don't always want Him to do it in the manner He chooses, because His process may turn over our ugly underbellies, revealing nasty, smelly parts of our lives and characters that we prefer to keep hidden. After all, aren't they better left unturned? I know I sometimes think so; why would I want anyone else aware of my secret, sinful past of sexual impurity, envy, defensiveness, pride, lying, deceit, and rage?

Why? Because with exposure comes healing and life. The Bible tells us so over and over again:

> Confess your sins to each other and pray for each other
> so that you may be healed… (James 5:16).

> David said to Nathan, "I have sinned against the LORD."
> Nathan replied, "The Lord has taken away your sin.
> You are not going to die" (2 Samuel 12:13).

Why? Because with exposure comes freedom from hidden guilt and shame, releasing our hearts from the dangerous hold Satan has on them.

> When I kept silent, my bones wasted away through
> my groaning all day long. Then I acknowledged my
> sin to you and did not cover up my iniquity. I said, "I
> will confess my transgressions to the LORD." And you
> forgave the guilt of my sin (Psalm 32:3, 5).

God doesn't expose your sin because He gets joy from seeing you ashamed or embarrassed by it. He wants you to become humble and repent of your wrongs against Him. But it's hard to repent of something you refuse to face in the first place.

Martha's (and Lazarus') Big Reveal

Fortunately for Martha, Jesus was willing not only to expose Lazarus' dead body, but to bring him back to life by His amazing, powerful call! John 11:44 states: "The dead man came out, his hands and feet wrapped with strips of linen, and a cloth around his face. Jesus said to them, "Take off the grave clothes and let him go.""

It had not been too late after all, even though all hope was gone. "Even now," Martha had professed earlier to Jesus. She now could see she had been right in saying so. Martha now knew that, because of Jesus' transforming power, she would have more years to see, hear, speak with, and love her cherished brother.

I'm not sure earthly reveals get any bigger than that.

The Spirit Helps You Trust

Reflect on the following statements in this chapter and apply them to your life by answering these questions.

1. *What if God wants us to throw out a last-minute, Hail Mary pass of faith?*

A. Why should you trust, as Martha did, that Jesus can heal your sickness, renew your spirit, or fulfill the loneliness inside your heart, even when it seems the opportune time for such blessings has passed?

B. Read Exodus 14, especially verse 14. When has God rescued you from a seemingly impossible situation?

C. The Holy Spirit produces faithfulness and peace in our hearts, among other fruits (Galatians 5:22-23). How can you tell He is increasing your quiet trust in God?

2. *Sometimes, we figure we're not all that worthy of saving.*

A. Jesus died for you while you were His enemy (Romans 5:6-10). He has proven that God loves you. Will you trust this love? How?

B. Check your heart: If you have a sin you believe God will not fully forgive, what is the basis for your belief?

C. Read 1 John 1:9. Does this contradict your belief or feeling that your sin is unforgivable? Explain your answer below.

(Hint: 1 John 1:9 says God not only forgives you, but He also cleanses you! If God considers you completely forgiven, you are indeed.)

3. *With exposure comes freedom from hidden guilt and shame, releasing our hearts from the dangerous hold Satan has on them.*

A. When someone confronts you about a character flaw or sin in your life, do you feel appreciative or defensive? Explain your answer.

B. What does Psalm 141:5 have to offer, considering the question above?

C. Why would Satan want you to fear someone else knowing about your secret sins?

D. Call a sister in Christ or a spiritual leader you trust today, confess to them the sin you've been so ashamed of, pray with them about it, and feel the relief confession brings (Psalm 32:3-5).

2

WHEN GOD CALLS YOU BY NAME
BY KENDRA MCCLURE

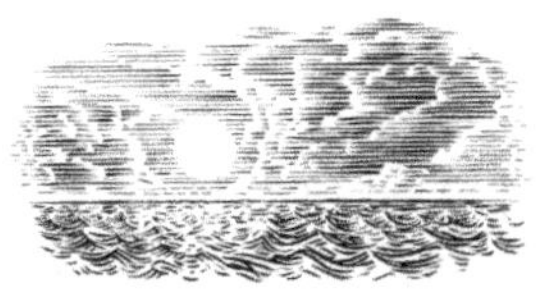

Jesus said to her, "Mary."
She turned toward him and cried out in Aramaic, "Rabboni!"
(which means "Teacher").
JOHN 20:16

How could Mary not have known it was Jesus?

I had asked myself this question for years whenever I read or listened to the story of Mary Magdalene encountering Jesus the morning He rose from the tomb.

I had asked, that is, until one very memorable Easter Sunday morning.

What Mary Heard in Her Distress

You know her story, from John 20: Mary, distraught by Jesus' disappearance from the grave, is looking around frantically for anyone who might know His whereabouts. She walks up to someone she thinks is the gardener, but is actually Jesus, and she asks: "Do you know where they have taken Him?"

In response, Jesus questions her: "Woman, why are you crying?"

She replies: "Sir, if you have carried Him away, tell me where you have put Him, and I will get Him."

Mary sees Jesus' face. She hears His voice. But she doesn't know it's Him.

How could she not have known?

It wasn't until I was reading Mary's story again on my 38th Easter, in April 2022, that the Holy Spirit opened my eyes to the truth God wanted me to glean from this passage.

Mary's (and My) Eyes are Opened

During this particular reading, the Spirit led me to ask myself some questions (and be convicted by the answers):

- How many times have *I* seen and heard God and not known it was Him?
- How many times have I looked around, wondering where Jesus went, distraught that He seemed to be gone?
- How many mistakes could I have avoided had I realized that internal nudges toward better choices were from Him?
- How many more praises of thanksgiving would I have lifted if I'd realized that blessings I thought I'd earned on my own merit were from Him?
- How could *I* not have known, in those moments, that He was standing right in front of me?

Then, as I read verse 16, He provided my long-awaited answer.

Jesus simply says, "Mary." He calls her name! Her eyes open. She realizes it's Him.

God opens our eyes in His time to reveal Himself to us.

What I Heard in My Distress

I don't think I would have ever understood this answer had I not heard Him call my name a few months after my *36th* Easter Sunday. And it happened in a place I never would have expected—a Positron Emission Tomography (PET) machine, a scanner that can detect cancer cells.

I was diagnosed with breast cancer in April 2020. COVID-19 had just shut everything down, and I was juggling three children under eight years old with a full-time job and household responsibilities.

I didn't have time to have cancer, and I initially approached my treatments as mere additions to my already full to-do list. After all, the prognosis had been positive, and as a person who grew up in a Christian family, I knew trusting God during a trial was the right thing to do. I didn't have any reason to think God wouldn't heal me though the chemotherapy, surgery, radiation, and hormone therapy my oncologist had prescribed.

But a short time later, a few tests pointed to the possibility that the cancer may have spread to my bones and liver. Spots that lit up on initial MRI and CT scans made me realize it's easier to trust God when the prognosis is good. The sudden shift from "things are looking good" to "the cancer may have spread" required a new level of faith. The thought that the cancer might win started to creep into my brain, and I realized that what I thought was going to be a sprint to a cancer-free finish line could turn into a marathon that finished at the gates of Heaven.

Complete Submission

I wasn't afraid to die. I knew I was a sinner who had been forgiven because God sacrificed Jesus, His only Son, for all of us. His grace and mercy saves us, even though we don't deserve it. It was the thought of leaving my husband and three children that I found excruciating.

My oncologist ordered a PET scan to determine if the spots were indeed cancerous. On the day of the test, I climbed into the scanner with a heart that wanted to trust everything I'd been told about God's faithfulness. I'd heard many sermons in my life about surrendering to God. He gave it all for us, so a logical response is to want to give it all to Him. I understood that cognitively, but I'd always struggled to put it into practice. I'd question whether I was really doing what God wanted me to do with my life or simply doing what I wanted to do, with the hope that my plan aligned with His.

All the struggling and questioning changed as they wheeled me into the machine. As I laid in the tube, completely still with my arms over my head, the words *complete submission* rolled over and over in my mind. Each time I heard them, I surrendered more of myself until an inexplicable peace washed over me. For the first time, I experienced what it feels like to submit my whole heart to Him.

God didn't audibly call my name that day, but like Mary, my eyes were opened, and I realized the peace I felt had come from Him. In that moment, He became more than something I'd just been taught to believe in. I'd read about, heard about, and sung songs about His grace, power, and mercy my entire life; but when I felt Him physically, He became real. I felt a closeness to Him I'd never felt before.

As I rose from the machine, I realized it didn't matter if the spots were cancerous or not. My life was now completely in His hands. Not just part of it. All of it.

My Big Reveal

I'm grateful I can say that the spots turned out to be benign, and I am now cancer free. I thank God every day for giving me more time with my family and for revealing Himself to me during my PET scan. Being diagnosed with cancer is something I would never have asked for, but I'm truly thankful to have had it, because God used it to teach me what it means to fully submit to His will.

Dear friend, has He called *your* name? If He has, have you answered His call? If He hasn't, take heart that He will do it in His timing, and remain faithful. When you do, His Spirit will open your eyes to God's love and purpose for you within your distress. Jesus says in John 20:29, "Blessed are those who have not seen and yet have believed."

Will you pray this aloud with me?

Heavenly Father,

We praise You for your power and thank You for your grace and mercy. You know that we miss Your presence, even when You're right in front of us, because You created us as imperfect beings in need of forgiveness that can only come through Jesus. We're grateful Your mercies are new each morning, and we humbly ask You to touch our lives according to Your will. Please give us the strength and courage to be obedient to Your call, whenever You choose to reveal Your plans for us.

In Your Holy name we pray. Amen.

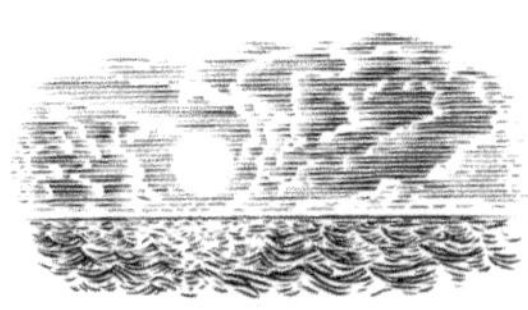

The Spirit Opens Your Eyes

1. How could I have not known that He was standing right in front of me?

A. Read John 16:7-8. Think of a time you went against the actions your conscience was directing you to take. Could you have been ignoring a conviction from the Holy Spirit?

B. Why might you not have recognized God's Spirit was reaching out to you?

C. How did ignoring His direction turn out?

2. I realized the peace I felt had come from Him. In that moment, He became more than something I'd just been taught to believe in.

A. Kendra experienced what I call a "Job moment," the moment she realized the complete sovereignty of God in her life and moved from head knowledge about Him to having heartfelt appreciation for His authority and closeness with Him (Job 42:5-6). When did you experience your "Job moment?"

B. Jesus acknowledged that He was laying down His life for His friends, the greatest expression of love (John 15:13). How does it make you feel to know you are Jesus' friend?

C. The Spirit helps you see you are not only Jesus' friend, but also His family member (Romans 8:16-17, 29). How closely do you connect with Jesus as your family?

3. I wasn't afraid to die. I knew I was a sinner who had been forgiven because God sacrificed Jesus, His only Son, for all of us.

A. Are you afraid to die, or like Kendra and Paul the apostle, do you believe death holds something greater in store for you? (Philippians 1:21)

B. Because your friend Jesus has died for you, you can come confidently before God's throne with your requests in times of sickness and trouble (Hebrews 4:16; Ephesians 3:12). What bold requests have you asked of Him lately?

C. Who among your friends needs to know that God sacrificed Jesus for them? Ask God for the opportunity and courage to share this good news with them.

PART II

NEAR YOU IN YOUR ROLE AS A WIFE

If you've been a wife for any period of time, you already know how challenging working at marital unity can be. Matrimony is not for the fainthearted; it's two individual personalities striving to caringly and consistently connect, collaborate, and cohabitate—and that's not easy! As the Apostle Paul said, "those who marry will face many troubles in this life" (1 Corinthians 7:28).

Those "many troubles" in the wife role can involve common issues, like making family-related choices or resolving minor disagreements. But you can experience tough challenges in this role too, like forgiving infidelity, loving through chronic illness, or—as in Sarah's and Abigail's cases—trusting in God through unwise, even life-threatening, decisions your husband makes.

By their examples of quiet trust and integrity through adversity, these women can teach you that even the troubles that threaten to overwhelm and destroy you are no match for the peace-giving Holy Spirit, whom Christ has sent to comfort you in all your troubles (John 14:16; Galatians 5:22-23).

3

SARAH: TAKEN BY OTHER MEN

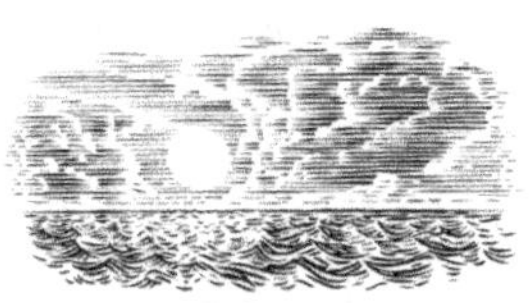

*Say you are my sister, so that I will be treated well for your sake
and my life will be spared because of you.*

GENESIS 12:13

As she was being led away to another man's harem chambers, Sarai turned to look back at the only man she had ever intimately loved and the only one she trusted in this foreign land—her husband, Abram. She had no idea what troubles lay in store for her.

Sarai's Troubled Beauty

The 66-year-old Sarai was so lovely to look upon that, once she and Abram arrived in Egypt, the king of Egypt desired her as a wife. He figured he could have her, too, because she was single and had come there with her brother. This was a deception, of course. Sarai was, in fact, married to her half-sibling, who had implored her not to reveal their marriage to anyone. Abram asked this of Sarai to save his own neck, not once, but at least twice, as recorded in the Bible (Genesis 12:10-20; 20:1-18). The second time Abram (whom God renamed Abraham) did this, Sarai (whom God renamed Sarah) was 90 years old. Good genes, indeed.

While it must have felt flattering to be admired for her physical beauty, it couldn't have been easy for Sarah to feel wanted and appreciated by a husband who could so easily release her into other men's arms. It reminds me of those men in the Bible who willingly let their virgin daughters or mistresses be gang-raped and terrifyingly brutalized by hordes of men in order to keep a male visitor safe[1]. The sinfulness of men made women into pieces of property back then, which was not as God originally designed the husband-wife relationship (Genesis 2:22-24; 6:1-3).

Added to this loss of respect from her husband was the shame Sarah felt for having a closed womb. For 89 years, Sarah had no children by which to honor her husband and to show she had been blessed by God. Her empty arms may have mirrored the emptiness in her heart.

Sarah's Submissive Faith

With such reminders welling up in her soul, Sarah surely had enough, right? Certainly she stayed the hand of the Egyptian slaves carrying her off to Pharaoh and defiantly declared her position as wife to the foreigner, Abram. Surely she harrumphed derisively about this "great man" they suddenly showered with gifts despite his having just thrown his greatest gift away. Surely her eyes threw daggers at Abram every time she passed him in the king's court, or she whispered her secret to one of her new servant girls in hopes of escape. Somehow, I don't think so. I don't think she did, neither as 66-year-old Sarai nor as 90-year-old Sarah.

It makes sense that God includes Sarah's name in the New Testament among the great pioneers of faith, one of only two women to receive this honor (Hebrews 11:11). It was her great trust in the providence of God that gave Sarah the strength to consider her husband's will before her own in his dealings with the kings of Egypt and Gerar (1 Peter 3:5,6). She patiently followed Abraham's instructions despite the personal danger. It would be that same trust in God that would strengthen her to bear Abraham's heir as a woman decades past child-bearing age (Genesis 21:1-6).

Imitating Sarah

Do you follow Sarah's submissive heart with your husband? For example, do you wait patiently and prayerfully for your man to make decisions about your family's lives as God's appointed leader of your household (1 Timothy 3:5) and then follow those decisions with a heart rested in God? Or do you doubt your husband's ability to make decisions, express your doubt through alarm, negativity, or criticism, and then begrudgingly get on board with him, if at all? Sadly, I sometimes make this latter choice with my husband Brian, letting fear get the upper hand in my heart at decisions he makes or opinions he expresses. However, whenever I do so, I delay our progress together or trigger unpleasant (albeit temporary) divisions in our unity.

Whenever we make this latter choice, we are not following in the faith of Grandmother Sarah, a trust in God that was so strong, she gently and humbly followed Abraham's leadership even when it didn't make sense to her and even seemed against her best interests or safety. Remember, even when we cannot audibly appeal to God about our suffering from spousal decisions (as Sarah's case may have been in Egypt and Gerar), the Holy Spirit helps our silent prayers reach God's ears (Romans 8:27), so we should take the concern to Him first before reacting, as often as we can. As we do, we should ask for the proper heart response to our husbands' actions.

Whose wisdom are we leaning on to guide our families, anyway—our husbands', ours, or God's? (James 3:13-17; Proverbs 3:5). We are Sarah's progeny when we don't let fear overtake the submission of our hearts to God (1 Peter 3:6).

Sarah's Big Reveal

By the way, did you catch it? Did you notice God's Holy Spirit hovering over Sarah's lonely, shame-filled void? He was there, moving, waiting for that big reveal. And what a doozy it was.

Each time Sarah was carted off to a foreign king's chambers due to her husband's fearful decision making, it was God Himself who rescued her. He gave those kings the drill: Touch her, and "you are as good as dead" (Genesis 20:3). He even stopped them from producing children until they let Sarah return to her true husband (Genesis 20:17-18). And each time she was rescued, Sarah was richer, both in finances and in faith, than when she was taken (Genesis 12:14-16; 20:14). Unsurprisingly, whenever I, too, have taken the *Sarah road* of quiet and submissive faith, God has shown me that my choice to do so was best and has rewarded my faith, putting me ahead of the game in both finances and faith in the end.

At age 91, Sarah would not only become a first-time mother, but she would also become the mother of the chosen people of God. Her 12 great-grandsons would become tribal leaders of one of the strongest and most enduring nations on earth, collectively named Israel after her grandson Jacob, to whom God would give this new name. And through Sarah's lineage, the Lord and Ruler of Heaven and Earth would be born as a human to save broken, sin-filled humanity, repairing the kinship between God and man forever.

Pretty smooth endings for a castaway wife, don't you think?

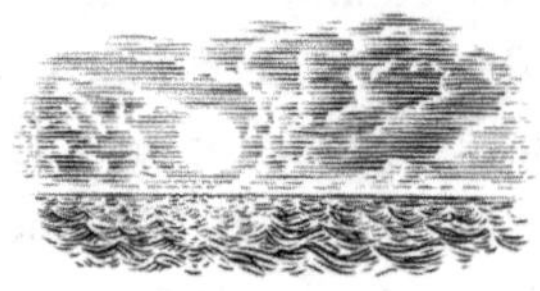

The Spirit Intercedes for You

1. *It couldn't have been easy for Sarah to feel wanted and appreciated by a husband who could so easily release her into another man's arms.*

A. Think of a time when your husband's actions led you to feel unappreciated, unloved, or unprotected. In response, did you lash out at him, tearfully criticizing, or quietly discuss how you felt with him, trusting God to handle the matter between you (Isaiah 30:15)?

B. Do you go to God first before responding to your husband's insensitive actions? Why or why not?

C. God wants to be actively involved in protecting and blessing your marriage union (Matthew 19:6; Mark 10:9). How often do you ask His favor on your marriage and on your husband's wisdom as the leader in it?

2. Each time Sarah was carted off to a foreign king's home due to her husband's fearful decision making, it was God Himself who rescued her.

A. Whom do you trust to get you out of difficulties and troubles at home?

B. To whom do you give credit when you successfully navigate a life storm (Psalm 50:15)?

C. The next time you share a triumph or blessing you have experienced, include God as its source.

3. *Each time she was rescued, Sarah was richer, both in finances and in faith, than when she was taken.*

A. What might have been the consequences to Abraham if *Sarah* had uncovered his identity as her spouse?

B. If God delights in you, He expects you to believe that He will reward you when you devotedly pursue a relationship with Him (Numbers 14:8; Hebrews 11:6). List some of His rewards to you.

C. God's plans include "prospering" you (Jeremiah 29:11). How have you seen His prospering favor in your life?

4

ABIGAIL: STAVING OFF DISASTER

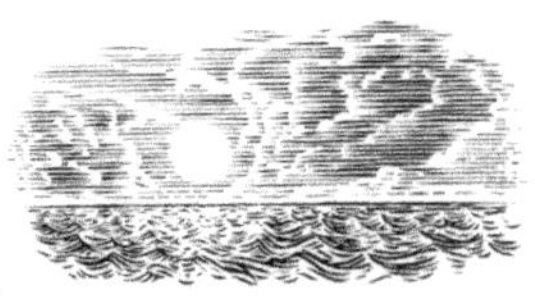

*"Now think it over and see what you can do, because disaster
is hanging over our master and his whole household. He is
such a wicked man that no one can talk to him."*
1 SAMUEL 25:17

She knew her husband could react stupidly, but this was deadly ignorance.

She knew he was stubborn and mean. But she never figured his churlishness would cost him his life and the lives of everyone in his household.

Yet, in just a matter of hours, death would likely overtake them all—all because Abigail's foolish husband, Nabal, couldn't find it in his heart to spare a few loaves of bread for rouge fighters who had been keeping his flocks and herds safe from marauders for months.

Trouble Looms for Abigail

Abigail had experienced his behavior before, too many times: Nabal's raging temper tantrums; his distrustful, snide comments to her, her parents, and the servants; and his arrogant boasting about his property. At times, he talked so much no one could get a word in edgewise, and he stingily shortchanged his trading partners. With every ignorant act or berating insult, Abigail would look upward in silent prayer. Could this man she had been given to in marriage so long ago ever change his tune? Could he at least try to be a little kinder? Perhaps she could even come to find him attractive on the outside if he didn't always act so ugly on the inside. And yes, Nabal seemed to grow uglier with each passing year.

But this time, he had taken things too far. This time, Nabal had insulted God's anointed king-in-waiting, David, son of Jesse. Nabal had coldly refused to give even a drop of water to the men David had sent asking for a little help. ("Whatever you can find for us, we'll gratefully receive," they had cried.) Nabal had even told them they were probably serving a lawbreaking, fugitive slave, to boot. What else could they have done after that beastly drubbing but head back for camp?

If only I had been there to hear their request the moment they arrived, Abigail thought, they would not have left empty-handed! How could Nabal put us in jeopardy like this? Thank God our steward has come to tell me about his rude reply. Abigail knew she could waste no time lamenting her situation; she had to act swiftly for the chance to repair the damage Nabal had inflicted and save her family.

Abigail the Quick Thinker

So, hurry she did. She sent a buffet ahead of her, strapped to donkeys, while she followed closely behind the servants who knew where David and his men were hiding. Suddenly, she saw God's anointed leader and about 200 of his men rounding a hill, headed straight for her town, swords at their sides. They stopped when they smelled the roasted lamb and bread, saw the raisin cakes and wine, and heard the appeals of a beautiful woman who was bowing as she approached them.

"Please pay no attention, my lord, to that wicked man Nabal. He is just like his name—his name means Fool, and folly goes with him," Abigail began as she approached David. "I didn't see your servants make their request, my Lord. Your servant would have not sent the men away empty. Please don't bring guilt on yourself by shedding innocent blood in revenge, for you are God's anointed king. And please remember me when you come into your kingdom," she begged (1 Samuel 25:2-42, paraphrased).

Imitating Abigail's Heart

In this scenario, you are Abigail, and Jesus your God-Anointed King. Are you approaching Him with the best of what you have available to offer Him—your time, talent, money, energy, and wisdom? Do you bow continually before Him in prayer, or do you barely pray at all? Do you openly acknowledge that He holds your past, present, and future in His hands[1]?

The thief on the cross did. Recognizing his demise was imminent, he, too, like Abigail, found the words to say to appease God's Anointed Son, the One he finally recognized as The King: "please remember me when you come into your kingdom" (Luke 23:42). As Jesus reveals in John 14:6, He is your only route to connection with the Father, and every knee, even those of earth's rulers, will eventually bow before Him, the Lord of lords (Romans 14:11).

Abigail's Big Reveal

By the way, did you catch the Holy Spirit hovering above Abigail as she bowed at the feet of David that day? He had been hovering the entire time she dealt with Nabal's behaviors too. And now was the moment of her big reveal.

After doing damage control with king-elect David, Abigail returned home to find her husband had partied himself into a drunken stupor. The next morning, she reported to Nabal what had transpired and just how close he had come to being annihilated.

At that very moment, Nabal suffered a stroke and fell into a coma! Ten days later, he died. Learning of her husband's fate, David soon called on Abigail and asked her if he could have her hand instead. In less than a fortnight, Abigail went from being the wife of a fool to being the bride of God's next anointed king of Israel. Queen Abigail.

And that's what you and I turn into, sister, as we bow before King Jesus. *Royalty.* Through faith and humble obedience to God, we become the Bride of Jesus Christ Himself; we become wife to the Lamb of God (Revelation 21: 2-9). We have become daughters of God

Himself, a royal line of priestesses (1 Peter 2:9).

And just as David sent for Abigail and took her to live with him the rest of her life, so your King will soon return for you, give you a new body, and receive you to live with Him forever in the beautiful home He has prepared just for you (John 14:3). And the Spirit will be there to rejoice with you (Revelation 14:13). I don't know about you, but I can hardly wait.

The Spirit Protects You

1. *Abigail knew she had to act swiftly for the chance to repair the damage Nabal had inflicted and save her family.*

A. Read Job 32:8-9. God's Spirit dwelling in you brings you wisdom. How does the Spirit's wisdom protect you in trouble, as it did Abigail?

B. When your husband makes decisions that threaten your family's well-being, to whom do you turn first to mitigate the threat and repair the damage?

C. Like Abigail did with David, be swift to mend things with the Son and submit to His authority (Psalm 2:10-12). You do not know when He will return.

2. *In this scenario, you are Abigail, and Jesus, your God-Anointed King.*

A. Abigail bowed before David in front of everyone. In what ways do you openly acknowledge Christ as ruler over your life?

B. How often do you bow before Jesus the King on behalf of your family's souls?

C. Are you giving your very best to the Lord like Abigail? What gifts are you holding back in service to the Lord?

3. *We have become daughters of God, a royal line of priestesses.*

A. When was the last time you reminded yourself of your royal station as the daughter of God? Why not write a prayer of gratitude to Him now for your holy inheritance?

B. As a priestess in the house of the King of Kings, for whom do you regularly make supplications and petition to God (2 Chronicles 30:27)?

C. Ask God to help you humbly fulfill the life of royal duty to God for which you have been chosen. Feel free to write out your prayer below.

PART III

SHARING YOUR HEART AS A MOTHER

Perhaps no role you and I hold is as challenging as "mother." Our mother-role troubles start as early as those first childbirth contractions (Genesis 3:16), and they certainly don't stop there. I remember hearing an old saying that, before they're born, children weigh heavily on our bodies; afterwards, they weigh heavily on our hearts.

These next two Bible stories reveal what those before-and-after troubles might look like. Hannah's "before" challenges center on her desperate desire to become a mother in the first place, while Rizpah must endure the ultimate "after" tragedy no mother wants to face: the death of her sons. Tuning in to the heavy hearts of both women, God moved in His time to answer their souls' troubles.

Let their stories show you how close God's Holy Spirit hovers over the heart of a mother. After all, He completely understands what it means to cherish and desire the best for all His beloved children.

5

HANNAH: GIVING A CHILD TO GOD

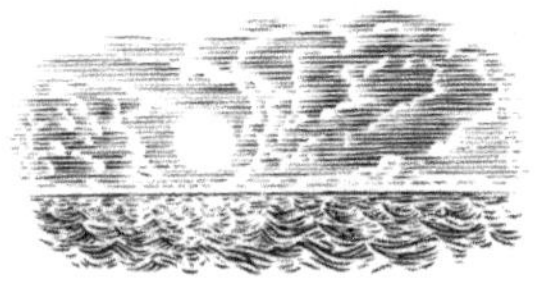

In her deep anguish Hannah prayed to the Lord, weeping bitterly.
1 SAMUEL 1:10

Whose child was he, anyway? Hannah reminded herself, as she folded the little coat she had sewn for her young son, Samuel. She knew the answer: He's God's, not mine.

Hannah tucked Sam's coat gently into a burlap sack, hoping she had made the garment large enough for him to wear comfortably. After all, it had been a whole year since she last held him, kissed his sweet little face, caressed his willowy hair. Perhaps he had grown faster than she had estimated.

Letting Go

Oh, how Hannah's heart beat faster with every thought of seeing her baby boy again! How she longed to be able to visit him every day, to hug him, to know if he was feeling well or poorly, happy or sad. But she lived with Elkanah, her husband, in Ramah, far away from the Lord's tabernacle in Shiloh where they had left the young boy in the care of Chief Priest Eli to be a student-servant for God's ministers (1 Samuel 1:28;2:19). Hannah recognized how impractical her longing was; Shiloh was well over 1,000 miles away, and it took many days to reach the town.

Nevertheless, her longings persisted. As Hannah prepared her own bags for this new visit, she remembered feeling almost inconsolable on that first night traveling back to Ramah without him! But there was no way she was going back on her promise to give Samuel, her miracle child, to God. In deep distress and through tears, she had once prayed:

"LORD Almighty, if you will only look on your servant's misery and remember me, and not forget your servant but give her a son, then I will give him to the LORD for all the days of his life, and no razor will ever be used on his head" (1 Samuel 1:11).

Hannah's Faithfulness Rewarded

Hannah was so grateful God had heard her plea and removed her disgrace. No longer could her rival Peninnah, Elkanah's other wife, tease Hannah incessantly because she was barren. No longer did Elkanah need to feel sorry for Hannah and her longing for a child. In fact, just four months earlier, God had blessed her a second time; she smiled, holding her hand gently over the nearly imperceptible movements of a new baby in her womb.

"Give to the Lord, and He gives back a hundredfold,"[1] Hannah said to herself, as she, Elkanah, Peninnah, and her stepchildren set out on donkeys again for the long trek south to Shiloh to worship.

Gratitude for the Gift of Children

Unlike Hannah, some women are blessed with natural fertility. Some bear children so easily, the ability even seems supernatural.[2] Yet, whether children arrive easily or we must beg God for them, all children are His special gift to us (Psalm 127:3). It's only right for us to show gratitude for gifts, especially ones so precious. God expected the Israelites to show gratitude for fertility by dedicating their firstborn sons and reminding their children about Him continually (Exodus 22:29; Deuteronomy 6:7). After all, He had been their First Parent (Exodus 4:22).

He expects no different from us today. God still expects us to show our gratitude for His gift of children by turning their hearts and minds to Him continually.[3] Such re-gifting of our children to God is most critical during the very early stages of life, while their young hearts are easily encouraged to love God by their parents, whom they love most in the world.[4] The Word teaches us why we must train our babies so early: when they're much older people, they often cycle back to what we introduced them to about their First Father (Proverbs 22:6).

Re-gifting is a Life's Journey

Because the pull of the world and worldly things will be significant as they grow, our children may drift farther and farther away from loving their First Father as they age. Yet our continual teachings about God and prayers for them can act as a strong tether, keeping them from languishing out on the open sea of disobedience to Him forever. Despite the rough waves and winds they may face, the tether we build can allow Him to gently pull them back to His safe shores of truth and protective harbor of salvation. He loves them so much more than we'd ever be capable of loving them. So let's make the tethers sturdy, for His sake.

Once our children become adults, this doesn't mean our re-gifting them to God ends. We must continually dedicate them to Him through our prayers for them prompted by the Holy Spirit, our examples of faith, and our loving, gentle reminders to honor Him. We'll need to do this for as long as we live, here and beyond.[5] We must keep returning to the temple like Hannah did, holding out to them the godly garment of Christ by our example of lifelong service to Him, hoping they will choose to put on that covering for themselves and keep it on (Philippians 2:16 KJV).

I'm betting the Holy Spirit encouraged Hannah to pray for Samuel that day, and every day. After all, He knew the plans God had for the boy. What a beautiful big reveal He witnessed after Hannah re-gifted her child to God!

Hannah's Big Reveal

Hannah's boy Samuel grew to become one of the most trusted and renowned prophets of his day, the last of Israel's pre-kingdom judges. While still a boy, he prophesied the capture of God's covenant ark and the removal of Eli and his sons as priests (1 Samuel 3:10-19). As a young man, he served his nation as prophet-priest-ruler (an archetype of Christ): He led the Israelites out of 20 years of Philistine oppression and into a long stretch of peace, raising his Ebenezer stone to mark God's battle victory (1 Samuel 7). In Samuel's later years, God charged him with anointing Saul and David, Israel's first two kings. Finally, God specifically named Samuel as one of only two Israelite leaders worthy enough to dissuade Him from rejecting the rebellious nation (Jeremiah 15:1).

Meanwhile, Hannah gave birth to five more children whom she raised with Elkanah (1 Samuel 2:21). Scripture tells us she earnestly prayed again, this time praising God for His mercies in removing her disgrace and silencing her critics; this prayer was also recorded for the ages and even includes a prophecy about Christ (1 Samuel 2: 1-10).

Here's one last note to encourage you: In what town would Samuel "the Seer" establish his office as judge, raise his family, and be buried? It was in Ramah[6], where his mom lived. God brought Hannah's firstborn, the one He had given her and that she had re-gifted to Him, back home into her arms once again.

Hannah couldn't outgive God. Neither can you.

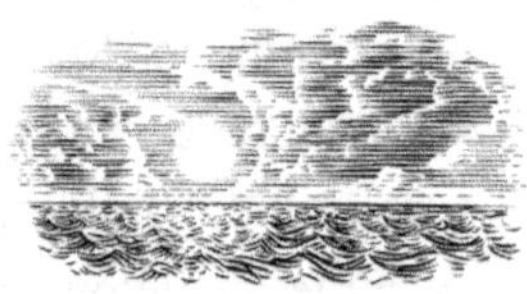

The Spirit Prompts You to Pray

1. *It's only right for us to show gratitude for gifts, especially ones so precious.*

A. Read Psalm 127:3. Do you consider your children as a gift or a burden to carry? They can often sense which one you feel, even without words. Make this a matter of prayer by recording below and on the next page the giftedness of each of your children.

B. How can you begin to express your thankfulness more often for God's gift to you of children?

C. If you don't have children, in what ways can you become a mother through the Spirit now, even as you wait for God to fulfill your physical longing through childbirth or adoption? (Jesus defines true motherhood in Mark 10:29-31 and Matthew 12:46-50, while Paul sets an example in 1 Corinthians 4:15.)

D. Whether barren or fruitful in childbirth, give thanks for your circumstances. Doing so stokes the Spirit's fire within you (1 Thessalonians 5:18-19).

2. Yet our continual teachings about God and prayers for them can act as a strong tether, keeping them from languishing out on the open sea of disobedience to Him forever.

A. Your godly protection over your children includes praying in the Spirit continually on their behalf (Ephesians 6:18). What does the Spirit prompt you to ask God for regarding your children?

B. Why should you continue teaching and encouraging your adult children about God?

C. How much more does God love your children than you? (See 2 Samuel 12:24-25.)

3. *Hannah couldn't outgive God. Neither can you.*

A. Hannah received many more children than she asked God for (1 Samuel 2:20-21). In what ways has God supplied you in abundant measure?

B. In Luke 6:38, is Jesus only speaking of finances? Explain.

C. Bless God with something today, whether your time, money, or service. See how He returns the blessing. Indicate below how you will bless Him today.

6

RIZPAH: PROTECTIVE EVEN IN DEATH

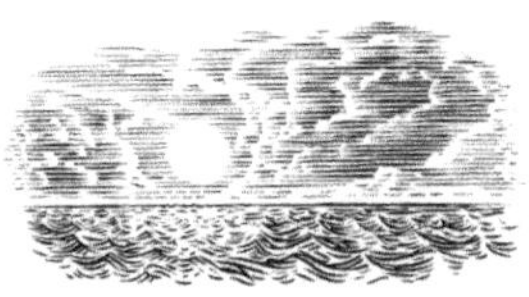

David brought the bones of Saul and his son Jonathan
from there, and the bones of those who had been killed
and exposed were gathered up.

2 SAMUEL 21:13

I have long been fascinated by Rizpah. After covering a nearby stone in sackcloth, Rizpah sits on it and watches her two sons, Armoni and Mephibosheth. They have just been hanged. Five of Rizpah's step-grandsons also hang dead on poles next to them (2 Samuel 21:8-9).

She shoos away buzzards from their rotting flesh in the sweltering heat. She fights off wild beasts that growl at her during the lonely, dark nights. She stares into her sons' faces, once full of light and laughter, now gray and lifeless. Eventually, Rizpah smells their decay, hears their maggots, and watches her precious young men slowly liquefy into nothing but skeletons.

Through strong winds, pouring rain, blazing sun, and rough, broken sleep, Rizpah sits, keeping vigil over her beloved sons' bodies. Not for a day, not for a week, but for five months. During a famine.

A mother's love never stops protecting. Or at least wanting to.

The Spirit Sees the Courtesan's Pain

Rizpah has already seen her share of grief. As a very young woman, she is taken to become a concubine for Saul, Israel's first king, used only to please him sexually and live in secondary status to his wives. Then, after bearing him two sons who would never be given real legitimacy as heirs, Rizpah loses Saul, who is killed in battle.

Earlier, at one point during his reign, Saul nearly annihilates the Gibeonites, a Canaanite community whom the Israelites had promised never to destroy.[1] Now, years later, to avenge Saul's gross misdeed and bring the land of Israel out of famine, David, Israel's newly installed king, grants the few Gibeonite survivors their request: He turns seven of Saul's sons over to them to be killed. Armoni and Mephibosheth are the first selected to receive this gruesome death sentence.

Her misery complete and her worst fears realized, Rizpah now wails on a cloth, wanting only to give her sons a proper burial and bring their lives some memorial dignity. And if she must, she'll die trying to get it for them.

The Awful Pain of Losing a Child

Many mothers know all too well the awful pain Rizpah was feeling, the troubling time that was threatening to swallow her whole. Over recent years, several of my female family members, friends, and acquaintances have experienced the death of a child, the scar across their hearts a still-constant reminder of the once-gaping wound inflicted at their moment of loss. It is that hug left ungiven, that smile left unseen, and that laugh they can no longer hear that haunts them. It is that enormous soul ache which, though tempered by time, will never go away because of the tender love it has replaced. I cannot begin to imagine what Rizpah was suffering and what my friends must suffer daily, nor do I ever hope to be called to bear what these mothers have had to bear.

Surely, this pain doesn't fall in the category of those "light and momentary troubles" that Paul talks about in 2 Corinthians 4:17! Instead, it weighs like a boulder under which a mother's soul must still navigate life.

Surely the Holy Spirit wasn't hovering here, watching an anguished paramour weep on a rock, was He? Yes, He was here too, waiting. Even here, with Rizpah.

Broken, but Not Forgotten

Like Rizpah, you and I can be tempted to think God has gone blind to our tears and deaf to our prayers. We can feel as though He has angrily thrown us aside because of our past sins, refusing our requests for deliverance from grief, loneliness, illness, or despair. And sometimes, these feelings of abandonment can last for years. (I call these feelings transformation process pangs; see the "Troubles, Transformations, and Big Reveals" section on page 7 for an explanation.)

Yet there's something we must remember about God. Yes, He does get angry with our sin, but He doesn't *stay* angry for long, nor does He give us all the punishment we deserve for our wrongs against Him. (And yes, every sin you and I commit or have ever committed wrongs *Him.*)[2] Psalm 103:9, Isaiah 57:16, Jeremiah 3:12, Ezekiel 16:42, and many other passages in the Old Testament point to God's description of Himself as One who doesn't hold a grudge forever, even when He has severely punished us. His Spirit longs to forgive, come alongside in comfort, restore, and gather us close to His bosom. like a hen gathers her chicks under her wing (Matthew 23:37; John 14:26; Psalm 139:7-8).

God wants you to know that contrary to your feelings, He loves you. He removes the guilt of your sin, even when you must face long-term consequences because of it. His will is for you to be broken, not hopelessly crushed and feeling utterly defeated and useless to Him. King David's repentance and restoration after his adultery with Bathsheba and then murdering her husband Uriah reveal this about God: Even after punishing David for his sins by taking the life of his and Bathsheba's baby, God 1) kept David from a justifiable death sentence; 2) revealed His love for their next baby, Solomon[3]; and 3) allowed Solomon to build a majestic temple to honor God, one in which He made His presence known (Psalm 51:10-13).

I don't know about you, but this image of a slowly angered, quickly forgiving, and gently restoring God brings me great reassurance. No wonder Satan doesn't want us to keep such a vision fresh in our minds or to retain the knowledge that God's mercies are new *every* morning (Lamentations 3:22-23). Whenever we don't receive the help we need or the desires of our hearts at the times *we* feel we need them, the devil seizes the opportunity to build doubt in our minds about God's perfect love and forgiveness. He can't make us doubt God, but he can (and does) suggest reasons why we should question that love.

I wonder if these were the questions plaguing Rizpah's heart as she watched her sons' decaying bodies for months and months, with no one lending a hand to take them down or bury them. "Does Yahweh see me, a former mistress of a defeated king? Does He care? Until He decides to help me, I will help my sons, because I love them," she likely told herself. "I will not leave them."

Rizpah's Big Reveal

God does, in fact, take notice of Rizpah's deep love for her sons and even deeper sorrow. And in His own timing, He does not let her love and sorrow go unaddressed. Because of Rizpah's courageous protection, God moves the heart of a conquering king to remove the disgrace of her defeated king and their sons.

Like waking up with a start from a long sleep, King David springs into action when he learns about Rizpah and her months-long vigil over her sons' corpses. He retrieves Saul's and his eldest son Jonathan's bones from the brave men who had stolen them back from the enemy, burying them in the Kish family plot. And starting with Armoni and Mephibosheth, David has the seven descendants of Saul removed from their Gibeonite posts of shame and properly buried as well. They receive final dignity at last.

The Bible records that it was only after David appeases Rizpah's anguished desire to bury her sons, and not just when the Gibeonites receive vengeance for Saul's murders, that God finally answers prayers to remove the famine from the land. He waits to fully heal the earth until Rizpah's heart begins to heal.

What the Bible doesn't record is what happens to Rizpah after her tragic loss is appeased. Perhaps there is no need to do so. Rizpah's story of motherly love and protection has been recorded for the ages, a moving testimony to the deeply grieved but abiding hearts of mothers who lose their children, whether from war, sickness, or other trauma.

Perhaps Rizpah teaches us that a big reveal may simply be the realization that God has been with you all along through your suffering and that no matter our station in life, *all* of us are important to Him.

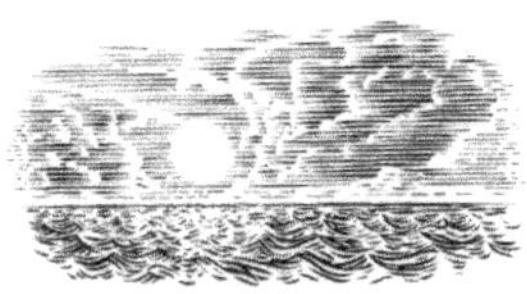

The Spirit Sees Your Sorrow

1. *Like Rizpah, you and I can be tempted to think God has gone deaf to our tears and ignored our longing.*

A. Why might God take months or years to answer the longings of your heart?

B. When God takes away someone or something you love or does not respond swiftly to your needs, what should your response be?

C. Read Psalm 56:8. What does this verse say about the value of your tears to God?

2. *Surely the Holy Spirit wasn't hovering here, watching an anguished paramour weep on a rock, was He?*

A. Called the Paraclete, the Holy Spirit comes alongside us, providing comfort and advocacy before the Father, the God of all comfort. (Read John 14:16, 26; 15:26.) Call on Him for comfort today.

B. Acts 10:34 shows us God's heart when it comes to seeing all of our griefs. But when might His Spirit turn away? (See Isaiah 59:2 for help with this answer.) Spend some time talking with God about anything in your life that might be making Him grieve. (Feel free to write a short prayer in the space below.)

C. What is your response when those who have offended you experience grief or trouble in their lives?

3. *He can't make us doubt God, but he can (and does) suggest reasons why we should question that love.*

A. Is loss or severe trial always the result of sin in one's life? Read Job 2:1-10 for the answer to this question and an example of what our response to trials should be.

B. Read 2 Corinthians 4:8-10, 16-18. How can you combat Satan's suggestions that God doesn't care about your grief and trouble?

C. Jesus, who is the Truth, called Satan the father of lies (John 8:44). As you grieve, be sure you know whose whispers to pay attention to.

PART IV

GUIDING YOU AS A DAUGHTER

As daughters, you and I sense keenly the influence and affection of our parents, especially our older female role models: mothers, mothers-in-law, grandmothers, aunts, and godmothers. In return, as God commands us, we typically seek to please our parents, obey and honor them, learn from them, and love them.

Nonetheless, as Jesus warned us, we will have trouble on this side of heaven (John 16:33), and the daughter's role is certainly not exempt. Perhaps troubling times fall externally on the daughter-mother relationship, such as the heartbreaking losses that Ruth and Naomi and college president Dr. Pamela Lau and her mother experienced. Or perhaps trouble develops from the relationship itself, threatening to unravel the very ties that bind you together with your mother figure. If so, you'll definitely want to read educator Dr. Plashan McCune's moving journey.

Whether your trouble in your role as a daughter comes from external or internal sources, you can gain comfort from knowing that God's Spirit wants to be with you, guide you through the difficulties, and help you grow from them. Listen to His voice. He is near.

7

RUTH: LOSS, LOYALTY, AND LOVE

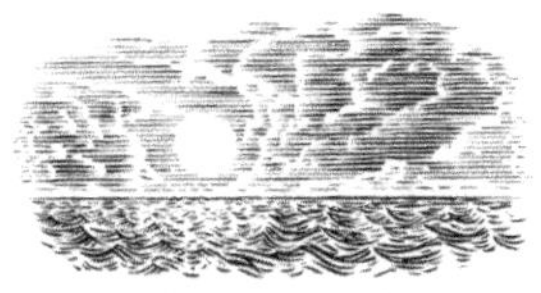

(To better understand this chapter, I encourage you right now to read the Book of Ruth in the Bible. It's a quick, fascinating read and it will provide many details that I won't have time to cover in this chapter.)

. . . . .

Placing her tiny baby in her mother-in-law's arms, Ruth felt as if she had just exhaled a sigh of relief that inflated the elder woman's lungs, bringing her back to life.

How Ruth had longed to see Naomi smile again like this and hear her familiar laugh once more! And although Ruth's journey to fulfill this longing was tortuous and formidable, she would have taken it all over again if she had to. For Naomi's sheer delight at this present moment would have made it all worthwhile, she thought.

Trusting Yahweh in Tragic Loss

Ruth loved and respected Naomi, a woman who had given Ruth warm, sincere affection and acceptance ever since she married

Naomi's son, Mahlon, who had recently died. While he was living, Mahlon, along with his mother Naomi, had taken time to teach Ruth about Yahweh, their God, the same God Ruth's own forefather Lot[1] had believed in but whom she had not been raised to know or fear. Ruth had come to understand and believe that their god was God, the One who created the heavens, earth, and mankind. Naomi had cared so much for Ruth. Naomi became dearer to Ruth than Ruth's own mother.

Later, Ruth would watch as a weary Naomi, her face stricken and grayed by sorrow, leaned on this very God when her own husband, Elimelech, died suddenly. In the midst of her awful grief, Naomi had prayed to Yahweh, trusting Him to guide her next steps. Ruth had admired her mother-in-law's steadfast reliance on God despite her bitter circumstances, and she desired to share such powerful faith.

Loyally Facing the Unfamiliar

Ruth had determined she would never leave Naomi to walk her grief journey alone! That's why Ruth had traveled back with her to Naomi's hometown, a land of unfamiliar faces and challenging risks. That's why, upon their arrival in Bethlehem, she had followed her mother-in-law's instructions to the letter after a stranger named Boaz treated Ruth kindly as she scrounged for food in a random field that turned out to be his (Ruth 2:19-3:6).

Did you catch the Holy Spirit hovering over that field? Yes, even in unfamiliar places that test us, the Spirit hovers, waiting, encouraging prayer, shining light on the next steps in our path toward the big reveal. You might even say difficult, unfamiliar places are His specialty.

A den of ferocious lions. A blazing furnace. An imposing, walled city. A battlefield facing a giant.

A virgin pregnancy. The cross. A prison cell. An island for the banished.

An oncology office. An unemployment line. A divorce law courtroom. The bedside of a dying child.

And Ruth's most risky, unfamiliar place? Lying at the bare feet of the very stranger whom she had just met and who had taken pity on her. In obedience to Naomi, Ruth had lain herself at Boaz's feet and uncovered them, offering herself as a wife to the much older man in the middle of the night, surrounded by a group of inebriated male grain threshers (Ruth 3:7-18).

No one can beat God for creative scenarios and risky suspense building. Or big reveals. Ruth's was quite the treasure.

Ruth's Big Reveal

Who was that tiny baby Ruth placed in Naomi's arms? That was Obed, her new son with Boaz. Obed would live to become grandfather to David, one of the greatest Jewish kings who ever lived, a man renowned for his loyalty and faithfulness to God.[2] As King David's great grandmother, and because of her own story of loyalty and love, Ruth would receive honorable mention within the genealogical record of Jesus Christ Himself, the great eternal King of the Jews (Matthew 1:5).

Even through the blinding fog of loss, our loyalty to and love for God can lead us back to a happy life.

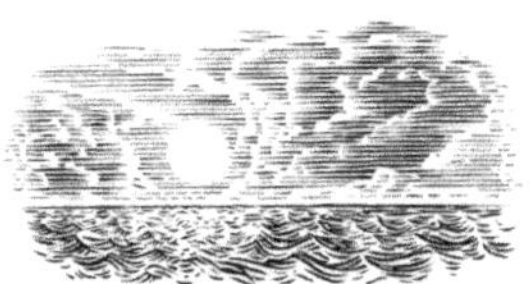

The Spirit Reveals Next Steps

1. *In the midst of her awful grief, Naomi had prayed to Yahweh, trusting Him to guide her next steps.*

A. When has grief made you feel as if you don't know where to turn next?

B. Read Psalm 56:8. One day soon, God will wipe away all of your tears (Revelation 21:4). But how does it make you feel to know He keeps track of your sorrows right now?

C. According to Matthew 5:4 and Psalm 34:18, why should you feel blessed, even as you mourn?

2. *Yes, even in unfamiliar places that test us, the Spirit hovers, waiting, encouraging prayer, shining light on the next steps in our path toward the big reveal.*

A. What unfamiliar spot in your life has tested you most?

B. Read Mark 13:11. How can you rely upon the Holy Spirit in risk-filled situations?

C. John 14:16 tells us the Spirit's chief description is that of Comforter. How has He comforted you in trouble?

3. *Even through the blinding fog of loss, our loyalty to and love for God can lead us back to a happy life.*

A. How do you avoid blaming God for traumatic loss in your life? (See Job 2:10 and Proverbs 18:10 for a clue.)

B. What Scriptures might Naomi have remembered to declare love for God in spite of her sorrow? (The stories of Abraham, Job, and Moses preceded her.)

C. God was willing to lose everything most precious to Him because He loves you (John 3:16). Write your response to that in the form of a prayer in the space below.

8

PRAISE INSIDE THE PAIN
BY DR. PAMELA LAU

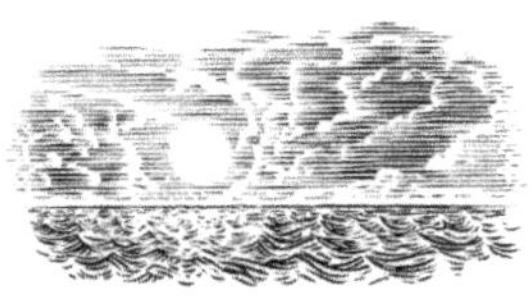

*"God is spirit, and his worshipers must worship
in the Spirit and in truth."*
JOHN 4:24

On Palm Sunday, Christians around the world remember the Lord's triumphal entry into Jerusalem, when crowds joyfully welcomed and heralded Him as the Messiah, laying down their cloaks and spreading palm branches on the road to honor Him. Unbeknownst to the crowd, the road to victory for the Lord required that He first pass through an excruciating death before He could be raised in a miraculous conquest over death, a conquest that promises the gift of life eternal for all who believe.

I remember my mother on a Palm Sunday some 45 years ago.

Mother's Life-Changing Crisis

Mother and I were in Darwin, Australia, foreigners in a land we did not call home. We had flown there a week earlier to be with my father. He had been flying from Singapore (our home) to Sydney, Australia, on business. During the flight, my father suddenly collapsed due to a severe heart attack. The pilot diverted the plane to Darwin so that my father could get to a hospital as quickly as possible.

By the mercy of the Spirit and through help from friends and strangers, my mother and I found our way to Darwin and spent a good week with my father. We treasured our time together. We talked a lot. Dad read and wrote letters to friends and office colleagues. By all accounts, he was recovering albeit slowly.

But Dad succumbed to a second heart attack on the morning of Palm Sunday. It happened while Mom and I were at Palm Sunday service. We did not know. There were no cell phones in those days. We found out only when we arrived back at the hospital after church.

Her Unforgettable Response

The nurse in charge led us—we were numbed with shock—into the room where my father lay. She then left us to give us privacy.

I will never forget my dearest mother's reaction. She reached out to touch my father with one hand. And in the Pentecostal style of worship that she was accustomed to, she raised the other hand toward heaven. Her first words? "Praise the Lord! Thank You, Jesus."

This was probably the most difficult moment of my mother's life. My father was the love of her life. He courted her during the Second World War while Singapore was occupied by the Japanese army. Together, they gave their lives to the Lord when I was about six months old. Together, they set up home and raised three daughters (I am blessed to be the second of three girls) in a home that honored the good Lord. Together, they served the Lord tirelessly, even helping to set up a new congregation. Together, they modeled love: faith expressions through the small things of daily life; selfless service in Christ's name; frugality and generosity; hard work and excellence. Together, they looked forward to retirement and travel.

Now, they would no longer continue life here together.

Her Reason for Praise

I cannot know exactly what went through my mother's mind that morning. Yet, in this moment of trauma, her first words consisted of praise. Praise while the tears flowed. Praise while her heart was filled with grief and pain. Praise even while she had unanswered questions and dashed dreams (Isaiah 61:3).

How could she offer praise in her heartbreak? Because she knew, without a shadow of doubt, the reality of the triumph that the Lord won that first Holy Week. He conquered death not only for Himself, but us all, too. Father had left us, but he was now in the presence of the Lord, the first in our nuclear family to go. Yes, way too soon, too suddenly, at least in our eyes. But he is now part of that "great cloud of witnesses" who are cheering us on as we who remain here on earth run the "race marked out for us" (Hebrews 12:1).

Her Legacy of Faith

The triumph of Palm Sunday remains even when it is no longer Palm Sunday on the calendar.

I remember thinking all those years ago: Tomorrow, when it is no longer Palm Sunday, I will think of the woman who by God's grace left an indelible mark on my life. I will remember how my mother walked each day with the Lord. It was a walk that reinforced the certainty of faith, a certainty that steadies one through the most difficult of times, a certitude that allows us to echo the confidence so aptly captured by the Old Testament prophet in Habakkuk 3:17-19:

> Though the fig tree does not bud
>   and there are no grapes on the vines,
> though the olive crop fails
>   and the fields produce no food,
> though there are no sheep in the pen
>   and no cattle in the stalls,
> yet I will rejoice in the LORD.
>   I will be joyful in God my Savior.
> The Sovereign LORD is my strength;
>   he makes my feet like the feet of a deer,
>   he enables me to tread on the heights.

The Spirit Moves You to Praise

1. *Her first words? "Praise the Lord! Thank You, Jesus."*

A. What "first words" might you have uttered were you in Pamela's mother's place?

B. What do you think her mother was thanking Jesus for at that moment?

C. The Holy Spirit is given to you to bring praise to God (Ephesians 1:14; Acts 10:45-46; Philippians 3:3). How often does the Spirit move your heart to praise *Him*?

*2. Praise even while she had unanswered questions and dashed dreams
(Isaiah 61:3).*

A. Jesus has provided blessings for you in your moments of grief. List
these blessings from Isaiah 61:3 in the space below.

B. How is gratitude an antidote for your unanswered questions and
dashed hopes?

C. Commit Habakkuk 3:17-19 to memory. (You can do this easily by
simply reading it through, aloud, once or twice every day for the next
30 days.)

D. How can you cultivate a heart like Habakkuk's?

3. *I will remember how my mother walked each day with the Lord.*

A. Read 1 Thessalonians 5:16-18. How can giving thanks during tragic circumstances benefit you and others?

B. What kind of example do you show your children for how to handle sudden tragedy?

(Read 2 Kings 4:8-37 and note the example of a woman whose faith kept her incredibly calm during calamity.)

C. What can you praise God for right now, in the midst of your trouble?

9

LIKE MOTHER, LIKE DAUGHTER
BY DR. PLASHAN MCCUNE

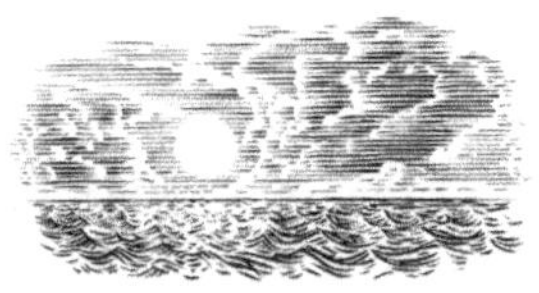

Everyone who quotes proverbs will quote this proverb about you:
"Like mother, like daughter."
EZEKIEL 16:44

All the pain that comes with being the daughter of an alcoholic existed in my life.

In my earliest memories, my mother would drop me and my two younger brothers off at friends' houses or extended relatives' homes, not returning for us or even contacting us for weeks at a time. Sometimes, staying with others was a blessing; we at least had regular food, hot water, and electricity. And during most of those stays, I was not being physically and sexually abused.

But whenever my mother would return to get us, sometimes drunk, sometimes sober, it was a different story. I was never sure what a day would hold for us.

If my mother was in a good mood, we could all talk and laugh and on occasion my brother and I would enjoy a good meal and clean clothes. But on a bad day, it was really bad. She would beat us for the slightest of infractions and sometimes for no reason that we could comprehend at all. The beatings were merciless. She would make us get naked, run a bath, and then put us in the tub and beat us with extension cords, belts, or broomsticks, whatever was handy.

You could say my mom and I have had a very complex relationship.

Escape, Danger, and God's Safekeeping

As I grew, ways to escape presented themselves. During more fierce beatings, I would end up running out of the house and into the neighborhood. This is how I learned that I could run. One Sunday morning, my mother had sent me and my brother out to start and warm up her car while she got dressed for church. My brother had decided he wanted to be under the wheel, and our tussling accidentally caused the car to shift and hit the car behind us. We knew there was no way we could avoid a beating for this error! We pulled the car forward, got out, and made a run for it.

We walked all day and into the evening! It was 9 p.m. and there we were—a 9- and 7-year-old, walking alone on the streets of the South Side of Chicago. Having no idea where we were going, we were scared. As we walked under one viaduct, a large figure approached us. I was so afraid. But as we attempted to pass him by, the man said to us, "Go home, it's safe; you will be okay."

For some reason, I felt a sense of comfort in his words at that moment. We turned around and walked back home. I am not even sure how we got back home; by this time, we were miles away. Even at that young age, I somehow knew that God was watching over me. I knew of God and prayed, but I felt then that He had spoken to me (Psalm 116:6) and was glad of it.

As a young teen, whenever I would run away in fear of my mother, I would do things to eat and stay alive that almost got me into trouble with the law, shot, or gang raped. In the midst of all this chaos, if it had not been for the Lord (Psalm 124) I would not be alive today. During this time, my mother sent me to live with an aunt in Kentucky, and there I was able to get back on track academically. I returned to live with my mother for the last two years of high school, and the beatings began again. In fact, right before Senior Picture Day, my mom left me with a black eye to sport in my pictures. Despite two very difficult years—miracles upon miracles—I still managed to graduate fifth in my graduating class. God had kept me again. Through all the pain, He spoke to me that my life would matter and that I would have a better life. He *kept* me (Isaiah 41:13).

It's a good thing He had been keeping me because, a week after graduating high school, my mother put me out of the house. I went to live with an aunt on the other side of town. Hers was a difficult environment to live in as well, but at least she didn't beat me. My aunt and my cousin's wife made sure that I could attend my orientation at the University of Illinois in Urbana, and I have not lived with my mother since. God had freed me *for good.*

God had plans for me, including earning college degrees, marrying a kind, loving man, and having two daughters of my own (Jeremiah 29:11).

Rethinking Mother-Daughter Interaction

Daughters. Before I had children, I would watch friends interact with their children and wonder whether I could love the way they loved. I wondered if I would beat my children the way my mom beat us or if I would practice time-outs, which I wasn't sure actually worked. What I did know was that, if ever I became a mother, I did not want to hurt my children the way I was hurt. I wanted to keep the good parts and leave the bad, to love them like God loved me. But what would that look like for someone like me, raised the way I had been raised?

After my daughters were born, my longing to be a good, godly mom instilled in me a desire to be very intentional with discipline. I didn't want to merely react but to respond with clarity as to why I was acting. I would pray and observe and pray some more. I would watch how others parented, Christians and non-Christians.

I soon realized that I didn't want to hit my children when I was angry, I wanted to teach them how to be obedient to God and their parents. I wanted them to know that when we disciplined them it was because we loved them and not because we were bigger or stronger or our perspective was more important than theirs. I wanted them to know that discipline was important but should be done out of love and care (Colossians 3:21). I wanted them to see God through me and not in spite of me.

Because of these desires, I decided that our parenting would be a consistent process that included discussion and Spirit-encouraged prayer. At times, this process felt challenging and, at other times, comical, especially when my husband had to try it on our then 2-year-old daughter, our oldest.

As my daughters grew into young adults, I would discover different challenges: How do I not kick my daughter out of the house when she makes choices I don't agree with? After all, I hadn't experienced how mother–daughter relationships even work past age 17. Still asking God for help all the time (as James 1:5 and 3:17 instruct), I followed the Spirit's guidance to make my daughters fully aware of my past and my challenges with my own mother.

Once, when my oldest daughter started making decisions that drove me crazy, we had a talk. We would often have talks, but none of them were as tough as this one. I admitted to her, "I don't know how to be a mother of a daughter older than 17; I barely knew how to do it up to now." We talked about what hurt us and what healed us, what would work for us, and what I needed from her to continue living under my roof, as a dependent of mine yet still an independent adult.

Now, I can't say everything has been smooth sailing since that talk. It hasn't, and it isn't even now that she is over 25 and a teacher living at home part time. I can't say that it has been a breeze for me and my younger daughter, a 19-year-old junior in college and future congresswoman, either. *Why get all these piercings and tattoos? Goodness!*

My Big Reveal, Bathed in the Spirit

However, thanks to the Holy Spirit dwelling in me, speaking to me, holding me, and interceding on my behalf, there are some things I *can* say.

I can say that my daughters and I are working things out. I can say that, although this motherhood journey has been fraught with challenges, some of my own making, we still pray through them. I can say that I still make sure God is in the center of my *why* and that love, not compromise or sentimentality, drives my speech or my silence.

I still may not know exactly what I am doing, but I am intentional about why I do or don't do things, and why I say or don't say things. I can say that, although my husband and I aren't perfect at any of it, we have been consistently doing our best and reflecting on how we can do better.

Oh, these challenges have kept me close to the Cross at times. Yet I praise God for His presence. He has taught me, poured into me, loved me, and shown me how to love my daughters in ways I had never known as a daughter but could grow to understand as a mother of daughters.

Finally, as I reflect today on our earlier commitment to be intentional, I can say we did okay. My daughters see I have lived a life committed to God and to His service. They see that I have tried to be a good wife, mother, daughter, sister, and friend. They see that, while I am not perfect and am still on this journey, I am not a product of my circumstances but a product of God's plan and intentionality in my life and in theirs.

I am confident of what my daughters see, not because I hope this, but because I have heard it from them. These are words my daughters used when writing their vows to my husband and me at our vow renewal a few years ago!

To stand and hear my two daughters speak such life and love to us on that day blessed me so much. I looked at them and listened to them, and I thought, *Look at what God has done! Oh, how He has been so faithful to me.* I started remembering times with my daughters: our talks, walks, and embraces; their baptisms; shared tears, joys, games, prayer times, and family fun nights; our saying "no" to some requests and "yes" to others. I hoped they felt my love and commitment.

Who knew that I, this imperfect daughter of an alcoholic mother, would have such an enriching, endearing relationship with my own daughters? Praise be to God for the things He has done for us through His Holy Spirit. When I touch my daughters, they know love and not fear.

The Spirit Guides Your Future

1. God had kept me, again. Through all the pain, He spoke to me that my life would matter and that I would have a better life.

A. Do you trust, as Plashan did, that despite your painful troubles, God's plan is to bring you abundant life? (John 10:10). Write your thoughts below.

B. Think back to your youth for a moment. When was God clearly keeping you safe, physically, emotionally, or mentally?

C. Read Psalm 113:9. Aren't you glad we don't have the last word on how our lives will matter? As Hagar did in her pain, hold on to the promises of the One who sees you (Genesis 16:10-13).

2. I followed the Spirit's guidance to make my daughters fully aware of my past and my challenges with my own mother.

A. Why might the Spirit want you to become transparent about your past painful experiences?

B. What did revealing her troubled past as a child of an alcoholic mother do for Plashan's relationship with her own daughters?

C. If you have trouble opening up about past parental abuse, speak with a reputable Adult Children of Alcoholics (ACoA) counselor or mental health therapist.[1] Doing so could move you forward to a happier future.

3. *Who knew that I, this imperfect daughter of an alcoholic mother, would have such an enriching, endearing relationship with my own daughters?*

A. Only God knows your end from the beginning (Isaiah 46:10), and His Spirit is gently guiding you toward it. How can you listen for His guidance?

B. In the Spirit, you are free from the control of sin, free to be more than your sinful past or troubled upbringing dictates. Reflect on 2 Corinthians 3:17 and write out your thoughts (or draw a picture) in response to that verse.

C. Have your children been negatively affected through your past troubles from a parent? Don't be afraid to apologize for your mistakes or reveal what led you to transfer your pain onto them.

PART V

YOUR SUPPORT IN YOUR ROLE AS A SISTER

Sisters: They can be our strongest allies or our biggest annoyances. In most of our experiences, though, sisters live somewhere between the extremes of ultimate treasure and outright nightmare!

Does your sister-role relationship lie on the loving end of this spectrum? Consider yourself blessed. Like Zelophehad's daughters did, you share sweet, Spirit-filled unity with your sister (Psalm 133:1-3). You learn to appreciate and rely on your sister's support and concern. Her love bolsters you as you face whatever troubles life blows your way.

At the unfavorable end of the spectrum, the sister-role relationship is not unity-building nor a bolster against winds of trouble. In fact, it can be the source of the trouble itself. This is what Leah and Rachel, the sister-wives of Jacob, experienced.

Both stories can teach you that, sisterly backing or no, God is the best source from which to draw your strength and support during troubling times. May His Spirit guide you in your role as a sister.

10

LEAH: STARTING FROM LESS THAN

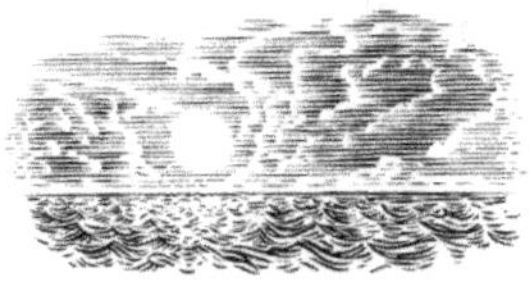

She conceived again, and when she gave birth to a son
she said, "Because the Lord heard that I am not loved,
he gave me this one too."

GENESIS 29:33

When someone you love doesn't love you, you can feel so low. But when the love you crave from them goes instead to a more attractive, popular, smart, or sophisticated sibling, you can feel even lower. Nonexistent, even.

That's how low Leah must have felt when her conniving father, Laban, passed her off in the dark as a new bride for his nephew, Jacob. Jacob had been celebrating all evening and was likely slightly drunk as he slid into his bride's tent, but he still was certain that he had just married Rachel, Leah's younger sister, whom he adored. That had been the agreement with Laban after all, or so Jacob had believed. The eager groom had no idea he was getting into bed with Laban's other daughter, Rachel's older sister, whom he cared nothing for. But when he woke up the next morning and turned over to kiss his new wife, there was Leah!

Years as "Less Than"

Yet, it was no surprise to Leah that she would be admired far less than her sister in her new husband's eyes. After all, she had spent years watching Jacob smile at Rachel, caress her face longingly, whisper niceties in her ear as he passed by, doing the labor required of his uncle to win her. Seven years, in fact. Jacob had been so excited he would get to marry Rachel, the years had passed by quickly for him. But not for Leah. Even as she felt glad for her sister's impending bliss, she longed to have someone love her in the same way. Yet that love never came. No suitor had ever called for her, secretly desired her, or even smiled her way.

And now, trapped in a loveless marriage, Leah could only observe with growing sadness that, although her husband would have sex with her out of obligation, he made love to her sister Rachel with deep desire and affection. Relegated to the sidelines of her marriage like a concubine, Leah must have felt so alone those first few years.

Yet Leah was not alone. The Holy Spirit was hovering.

Finding Her Value in the Creator's Eyes

Where, in your life, have you been viewed as *less than* in the eyes of someone important to you? Has it been in a loveless marriage like Leah's, with a spouse who hardly recognizes you or shows you the affection you crave? Was it with parents who favored a sibling over you and treated (or mistreated) you accordingly? It can be a sad, lonely experience to have friends or family members treasure your siblings while ignoring you, leaving you feeling less than. Any self-esteem you might have had at that time can start to plummet, as you're tempted to wonder whether there is, in fact, something about you that deserves to be treated with less affection.

At times during my early youth, I experienced this kind of loneliness. But, with time, I came to recognize the existence of One who did not consider me as less than anyone else in all the world. One who wooed me and who (as I daily prayed, "Lord, make me secure in Your love") helped me recognize and accept the most important love I ever had and could ever have. One who taught me through His written words that I was a treasured, special young woman to Him.

Rejoicing Through Rejection

Slowly, God showed this to Leah, too, and, under the watchful eye of the Holy Spirit, she began to long less to *receive* adoration from Jacob and to long more to *give* adoration to God, her true Husband. In her book, *When Women Walk Alone*, Cindi McMenamin describes Leah's transformation beautifully:

> We're told in the Bible that God saw that Leah was unloved, so He allowed her to conceive a child (Genesis 29:31). When Leah bore her first son, she said "It is because the LORD has seen my misery. Surely my husband will love me now." But Jacob's love didn't follow. [...] After giving Jacob a fourth son, and seeing that her husband still favored Rachel, Leah simply said, "This time I will praise the LORD (Genesis 29:35). I love how Leah's focus finally shifted.[1]

I've seen women wrapped so tightly in desire for their husbands' adoration or attention that, when this attention ended suddenly due to death or divorce, the women's lives were nearly shattered. Alternatively, I have seen women who, instead of shattering in despair after a husband's death or infidelity, made it a point to comfort other family members and friends through their loss, because the women fully understood that they were still highly valued and loved by the Lamb, their True Husband. Because He was with them, each of these women walked through their grief like a boss! So did Leah.

What's more, the Spirit moved Leah's heart from unfulfilled longing to godly praise *during* her troubling times. She rejoiced in the *midst* of the rejection, not after it. And this heart change, while important, was just *part* of the process of Leah's transformation. It was only the beginning of her big reveal.

Leah's Big Reveal

God made sure it would be less-than Leah (not much-preferred Rachel) who would be buried in the Cave of Machpelah, the renowned family tomb of the Jewish patriarchs—a position of honor (Genesis 49:31). Jacob would ask to be buried with *her*. In contrast, Rachel, who died giving birth to her second son, would be buried in an unmarked tomb on the side of the road near Bethlehem, the precise location of which is contested to this day.

Furthermore, although God made Joseph—Rachel's son who was once enslaved in Egypt—rise in prominence there to rescue the Hebrews from deadly famine, He made Jesus—a descendant of *Leah's* son Judah—leave Egypt as a baby and rise in prominence as the final King of the Jews to rescue mankind from spiritual death forever.

You may feel you are less than in the eyes of men, but you're *never* less than in the eyes of Almighty God, who has no respect of persons (Acts 10:34 KJV) and has the final say on how our futures unfold. It's His opinion of us that truly counts.

The Spirit Reveals Your Value

1. *Slowly, God showed this to Leah, too, and, under the watchful eye of the Holy Spirit, she began to long less to receive adoration from Jacob and to long more to give adoration to God, her true Husband.*

A. Take an honest assessment: Do you spend more time seeking praise and acceptance from humans or giving praise to God? Explain your answer below.

B. Who changed Leah's mindset about gaining Jacob's heart?

C. Read Lamentations 3:22-23. Why would God's love for you hold greater value than a family member's?

D. Take a moment to praise Him for His love.

2. *God made sure it would be less-than Leah (not much-preferred Rachel) who would be buried in the Cave of Machpelah, the renowned family tomb of the Jewish patriarchs—a position of honor.*

A. Read Matthew 20:16, 19:30 and 1 Corinthians 1:27. Considering what you read in those passages, what can we learn about God from Leah's and Rachel's outcomes?

B. Genesis 25:23 and I Samuel 16:7 reveal how God sometimes selects a younger son over the elder—the one expected to receive the best of the inheritance. What similar instances of His selection method do you find in the Scriptures?

C. God saw Leah was not loved by Jacob and ultimately showed her just how loved she was, by Him. How long can you wait for God to show His favor to you, when you are not feeling loved?

3. *You may feel you are less than in the eyes of men, but you're never less than in the eyes of Almighty God, who has no respect of persons (Acts 10:34).*

A. Read Ephesians 5:25. Christ gave Himself up for you, because He loves you. What other scriptures show you are a beloved daughter of God, His treasured possession?

B. Sometimes, we feel less than others who have more wealth, talents, opportunities, or position. Romans 8:10 says God's Spirit lives in us. How does the Spirit want you to view yourself with regard to others?

C. Consider Psalm 73:2-6 and Galatians 6:3-5. How do you reconcile these reflections with Paul's commands in Romans 12:3 and Philippians 2:3?

11

ZELOPHEHAD'S DAUGHTERS: A UNITED FRONT

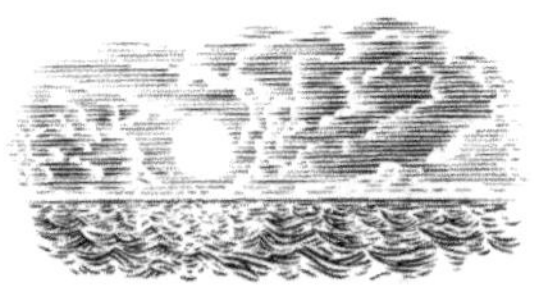

"And the Lord said to him, "What Zelophehad's daughters are saying is right."
NUMBERS 27:6-7

They faced want and destitution sitting on a gold mine. They held everything they needed to survive with no claim to hold it.

But they did have each other, these sisters, daughters of Zelophehad. And while the bond of sisterhood may not have seemed enough to shield these five women from impending poverty, it was sufficient to bolster them and shield their hearts from despair.

Those hearts were still reeling from grief as they approached Moses and the priests, their judges. Mahlah, Noah, Hoglah, Milcah, and Tirzah had just lost their dear father. He was an imperfect man, yes, but one who had cared for them, doted on them, treasured them. And because Zelophehad loved his daughters, he had trained them to embrace hard work. Yes, hearty and tough, these women could work the land with the best of men. They would certainly hold their own— and prosper—if given the chance. Their dad had taught them well.

No Rights, but a United Front

As Israelite customs would have it, only men could inherit land and property from their fathers. And when a man had no sons, as in Zelophehad's case, the inheritance passed on to the closest male heir, not to daughters. In fact, "in Israel a woman was treated like the property of her father, and was then transferred to her husband via a bridal payment".[1] It's the same reason Boaz needed to redeem the property of the widow Naomi and her daughter-in-law Ruth; Naomi, as a widow, required a male relative to help her keep her husband's name alive among the Israelites.

Well, they may not have had the right to inherit the land their dad had been granted years earlier, but that fact was not going to stop these sisters from trying to attain it. They knew Zelophehad's name would be erased from among his people if his property and land promise were absorbed by some male relative. So they brainstormed and came up with a plan of action. They put their heads together to devise the means of attacking what seemed like an insurmountable dilemma. Whichever way they would tackle this problem, they would tackle it together—as one voice, one heart speaking truth to reason. And reason they must, with their world's leading men (Numbers 27:1-7).

The Power of Unity

Unity. There's just something formidable about unity in getting the job done, something powerful in it to reach dreams. Think of what labor, suffrage, civil, and human rights movements around the world have accomplished through solidarity. Even God took notice of early man's united effort to reach Him via a telescoping tower, so much so that He mixed up their language, confounding this unison so men would abandon a futile effort that likely would have killed them (Genesis 11:1-9). For good or evil, a plan backed by unity cannot easily be ignored; it must be reckoned with.

So it was with the sisters' plan. Together, they would seize an opportunity when Moses, the chief priest, the leaders, and the entire assembly of the Israelites were gathered in one place. And together, the *six* of them would stand up and plead their case to retain their father's inherited property.

The United Six and the Big Reveal

Wait, six? Weren't there only five sisters? Yes, but the unseen Holy Spirit was hovering in their midst. He had been with the sisters in their desert wanderings with the Israelites, had walked them through the sorrow of losing Zelophehad, and now was affirming their courage and watching as their verdict unfolded, the verdict God Himself delivered to Moses:

> "What Zelophehad's daughters are saying is right. You must certainly give them property as an inheritance among their father's relatives and give their father's inheritance to them" (Numbers 27:6-7).

Certainly. They're right, God says. Right to have asked, right in their reasoning, right in the heartfelt, unified way they decided to honor Zelophehad and keep his memory alive.

So you *must* give, God concludes. Give these courageous sisters their father's inheritance among Manasseh's tribe. Give them back the dignity and worth of the family name. Give them a means of independent sustenance for the generations to come.

So, Moses did.

In fact, these brave sisters' act paved the way for other Israelite daughters who had no male siblings. From that point forward, it would be the law of the land that, whenever a man died and had no sons, his daughters would inherit the property (Numbers 27:8).

What can unity do for you?

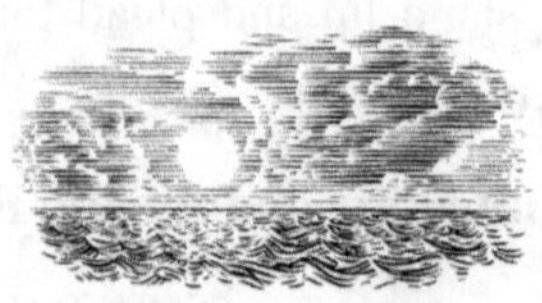

The Spirit Unifies

1. *Unity. There's just something formidable about unity in getting the job done, something powerful in it to reach dreams.*

A. Read Psalm 133:1-3. Think of a time you had sweet communion with sisters, physical or spiritual. How did it make you feel?

B. The Bible teaches there is strength in numbers (Ecclesiastes 4:9-12). Name some of unity's benefits found here.

C. Read John 17:20-23. What's the greatest effect Christian unity can have on the world?

D. Read Ephesians 4:3. What does this verse instruct you to do in regard to unity?

2. Wait, six? Weren't there only five sisters? Yes, but the unseen Holy Spirit was hovering in their midst.

A. Do you think the sisters together called on Yahweh for help before approaching their nation's leaders?

What would they have asked Him for?

B. God (Elohim) breathed power into the sisters' plan as the Holy Spirit covered them. Read 2 Timothy 1:7. Write out a prayer below, inviting the Spirit's power, love, and soundness of mind into your next collaboration.

C. The Holy Spirit is here to bring guidance and relief during all tough challenges, no matter the size or type. What does Hebrews 4:16 tell us to do during our time of trouble or need?

What trouble or need will you boldly ask Him to help you through today?

Ask Him now in a silent prayer or write out that prayer below.

3. *In fact, these brave sisters' act paved the way for other Israelite daughters who had no brothers.*

A. Zelophehad's daughters' story shows us that a united stand can have multigenerational benefits. Explore Genesis 11:1-9 and Joshua 6:1-27 for other examples.

B. There are many courageous women in the Bible, such as Philip's four unmarried, prophesying daughters (Acts 21:8-9). Name a few others in the space below.

C. Have there been any acts of unity that eventually benefited you? (Parental decisions? Human rights stances? A community of believers taking action?) List any that come to your mind.

Thank God for His foresight and providence.

PART VI

YOUR EXAMPLE AS A SERVANT

The greatest person who ever walked the earth said He came to serve (Matthew 20:28; Luke 22:27). If that fact doesn't show you the importance God places on adopting a heart of servanthood no matter your station in life, I don't know what does.

Serve yourself only and you will destroy yourself. This was the ultimatum for Esther, the Queen. Serve courageously as a leader even when others might destroy you for it. Judge Deborah teaches you how to do that. Serve others constantly with no self-care and you could destroy further opportunities for service. Even Jesus recognized this need (Mark 6:31-33), but it was one that entrepreneur Grace Darling had to learn the hard way.

The Spirit that hovers over and lives in you and me seeks to please God by helping others around us, particularly those within the body of Christ (1 Corinthians 12:1-11). Like these women, may we answer His promptings to serve, whether through noble feats or small gestures of kindness.

12

Esther: Daring to Confront

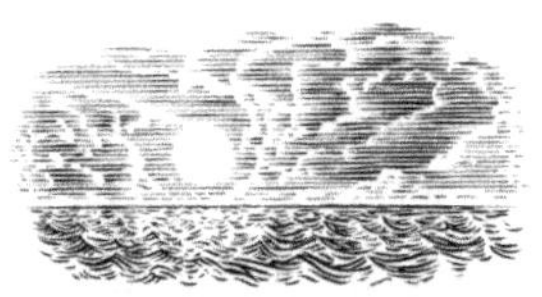

Esther said, "An adversary and enemy! This vile Haman!"
ESTHER 7:6

Mordecai's plan was simple: His young cousin, Esther, would present herself to the ruler currently subjugating her people and inform him that his most trusted vizier involved him in a plan as crooked as a witch's finger.

Of course, the ruler in question, King Xerxes of Persia, would likely order that Esther, his new wife, be executed for having dared present herself in his inner court without an invitation. Nobody could commit such a publicly impudent, lawbreaking act and get away with it unless the king granted them a last-minute pardon. And after all, hadn't Xerxes chosen Esther as his queen to replace Vashti, whom he deposed for public impudence toward him?[1]

Mordecai's Call for Courage

Esther's cousin Mordecai was the closest she had to a parent while growing up. After her parents died during the Babylonian occupation of Judea, Mordecai had taken Esther under his wing, caring for her like his daughter. She had fully obeyed his instructions and trusted his care for her.[2]

That's why it hurt her heart to learn that Mordecai was wailing, robes torn, and refusing to be consoled outside the palace gates.

Now the Persian queen, Esther had sent her messenger to discover why her cousin was in such distress. Now, she knew: Haman the Agagite, a high-ranking official who hated Mordecai, had just plotted to exterminate the Jews from Persia, using Xerxes' seal and the Jews' own neighbors to carry out his scheme.[3] "It is a heinous act that has to be revealed to Xerxes right away," Mordecai tells the messenger.

Faced with this new directive from her beloved Mordecai, however, Esther hesitates—perhaps for the first time in her life—to obey him. Alarm grips her heart. *Is God really saying I must die?* she wonders. *Could this even work?* She feels a little like Moses at the burning bush, preferring God send someone else to deliver the important message about His people to a foreign ruler (Exodus 3:11; 4:13).

Mordecai responds to Esther's trepidation and hesitation with faith enough in God's power for both of them. Through her messenger, he replies that he not only believes God will rescue the Jews, but that God has likely placed Esther, his young charge, in a position of great influence to bring about national deliverance.[4] "Sure, you may die if you approach your husband unsummoned," he reasons, "but you'll die for certain if you fearfully refuse to use your God-given power to help us, His people, at this crucial moment."

The Spirit's Call for Prayer

The Holy Spirit, who had been hovering over Esther all her enslaved, orphaned life, now encourages her not only to pray but to ask Mordecai to tell all the Jews in Susa to pray for her as well. For three days. Without eating.[5] Desperate times call for desperate measures, and when God's people fast and pray, He hears (Ezra 8:23).

Can you hear the desperation in Esther's and her fellow Jews' voices as they kneel before God seeking courage and deliverance? Like them, you and I can receive the courage we need from the Spirit to face any challenge, when we pray humbly to God in faith for it.

Indeed, the prayers of the righteous wield great power to bring about the Spirit's strength. The two go hand in hand. Paul, the apostle, knew this, In Philippians 1:19-20, he tells the church, "for I know that through your prayers and God's provision of the Spirit of Jesus

Christ what has happened to me will turn out for my deliverance. I eagerly expect and hope that I will in no way be ashamed, but will have sufficient courage so that now as always Christ will be exalted in my body, whether by life or by death." Never underestimate just how powerful and effective prayer can be (James 5:16).

During Esther's time of prayer, the Spirit reveals to her exactly how to tackle the crisis: She must daringly confront Haman in the king's presence. She must not simply run to the king and tell on Haman. No, she must look the chief vizier squarely in the face as she uncovers his wicked deed.

A sense of calm washes over Esther as she ends her days of fasting and petitioning God. *Yahweh has always been my cousin's hope and strength. He has long listened to Mordecai, protecting and providing for both of us,* she reflects. *It is worth sacrificing my life to preserve the children of Almighty God.*

God's Plan in Action

With this same peace-filled calm, Esther walks over to the king's inner courtyard and waits, unannounced and unsummoned, yet standing tall. Xerxes sees her. The king smiles, holding out his golden scepter of pardon, and invites her in. She invites him and Haman to her place for a meal, for two consecutive evenings.[6] She doesn't even know why she needs to invite that vile Haman to dinner *twice* before confronting him. But the Spirit knows. It's all part of Esther's big reveal.

Between Esther's banquet invitations, God does three things:

First, he endears the beautiful Esther to King Xerxes more than ever. Now, his heart filled with so much admiration for her, he wants nothing more than to please her as much as she pleases him.[7]

Second, God lifts Mordecai to a prominent place in Xerxes' esteem. The very next day, the king orders Haman to loudly proclaim Mordecai's excellence all over town, like a footman heralding the arrival of royalty. After all, nothing had been done to honor Mordecai for having uncovered an evil plot against Xerxes by his aides a few months earlier.[8]

Third, God lets Haman's own arrogance and hate prepare a super-tall gallows, one on which he and his own sons eventually would hang, visible to the entire city[9]. Haman has ordered the device to be built to kill Mordecai, but God has other plans.

Esther's Big Reveal

At her second banquet, Esther confronts her enemy, revealing to King Xerxes how Haman has threatened her life and the life of her people. In a fury, the king orders that Haman be hanged on the very gallows he had built for Mordecai. Not only was Haman to die, but the 10 sons he bragged so much about as well! Soon after, Esther tearfully begs the king to help save her people from annihilation. Xerxes does so by issuing a second edict that would allow the Jews throughout the kingdom to defend themselves against anyone who tried to kill them.[10]

By heeding the Spirit's guidance to pray and daringly face Haman, Queen Esther saved the Jews from total destruction under their Persian captors. Her courageous acts became the stuff of legend in Jewish history books, retold throughout the generations that have followed her.[11]

Esther teaches us we can trust our God to protect us whenever we call out mankind's evils against Him. Even when it's scary, and even if we must die holding out God's truth, we will have courage, because He's with us and it is totally worth the sacrifice (Esther 4:16).

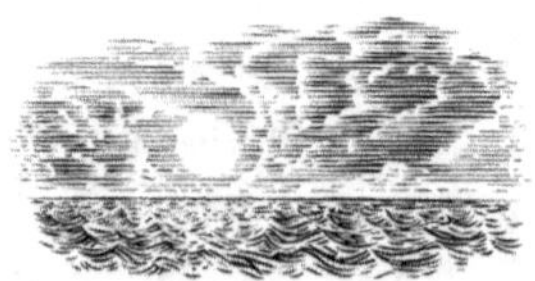

The Spirit Grants You Courage

1. *She feels a little like Moses at the burning bush, preferring God send someone else to deliver the important message about His people to a foreign ruler.*

A. When the Spirit calls you to be bold for Christ's sake, do you respond more like Moses (Exodus 4:13) or Isaiah (Isaiah 6:8)?

B. Like Esther, we can initially focus on our threatening situation instead of on our loving Sovereign Lord who is able to help us through it. Read Psalm 121:1-2 and Colossians 3:1-3. Where should our focus be during a crisis? And how can we move our focus to where it should be?

C. Despite your initial hesitation or objections, God is still willing to use you to fulfill His purposes, because He loves you (Psalm 138:8). Ask God for the courage and the will to do what He wants to do through you.

2. During Esther's time of prayer, the Spirit reveals to her exactly how to tackle the crisis: She must daringly confront Haman in the king's presence.

A. The Spirit will help you courageously hold out the truth despite strong opposition (1 Thessalonians 2:2). Pray for His support in any challenge you face.

B. Read 2 Timothy 1:7. What does the Spirit give us to counteract fear and timidity?

C. Other women from the Bible required courage to carry out God's will. Names like Deborah, Ruth, and Mary come to mind. What others can you think of?

3. *By heeding the Spirit's guidance to pray and to daringly confront Haman, Queen Esther saves the Jews from annihilation under their Persian captors.*

A. Read Joshua 1:9-11 and Psalm 18:29-35. What amazing things can God do with you when you answer the Spirit's call to be courageous?

B. Trusting in God as you boldly serve Him can save lives. Read the account of David's confrontation with the Philistines in 1 Samuel 17 and list some examples of how David trusted in God.

C. Read Jude, verses 20-23. Consider whom God's Spirit might be calling you to help rescue.

13

DEBORAH: CALLED TO LEAD

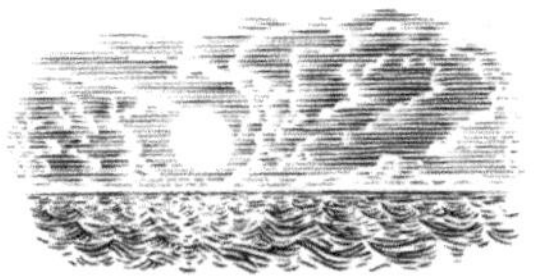

*"Villagers in Israel would not fight; they held back until I,
Deborah, arose, until I arose, a mother in Israel."*

JUDGES 5:7

*J*udging *the people's disputes is one thing, but this is war, the realm
of men. Must a woman now give the battle cry, too?* Deborah must
have wondered this as she stood before Barak, son of Abinoam, the
soldier from Kadesh she had just summoned. *Is there truly no man
willing and faithful enough to lead God's people in victory over their
oppressors?*

If you think finding godly, faithful leaders can be challenging these
days, you should have lived during Deborah's day.

In her day, the Israelites had become idolatrous and corrupt,
and God punished them by having Jabin, king of Canaan, and his
army commander, Sisera, subdue them for 20 years. Life was so
troublesome for the Israelites, they feared traveling along the main
roads or even drawing water from their wells (Judges 5:6,8,11 KJV).
Canaanitic terrorism had left Deborah's countrymen deficient in faith
and courage. It must have been depressing to witness.

Just a few years earlier, the Israelite elders had ascended the
Ephraimite hill country and asked Deborah to lead them as judge. At
the time, she identified herself as a mom, raising her kids and caring
for her family in the hills. Nonetheless, they desired to make her home

the Supreme Court over their disputes, as they recognized that she was a woman on whom God's Spirit rested, one who carried gifts of prophecy and wisdom. She was willing to serve God in this new role, and so the woman who referred to herself as "a mother in Israel" became the nation's judge (Judges 4:5, 5:7).

Called to Lead during Trouble

Sometime after Deborah became the judge, God revealed to her His plan to free her people from their long oppression. He planned to send a soldier, Barak son of Abinoam, to lead the Israelites in battle against King Jabin and Sisera. Despite the revelation to Deborah, however, Barak expressed little confidence that he could lead an army successfully against Sisera, his archers, and his fierce fighters in iron chariots. After all, Barak had only fellow foot soldiers from Naphtali and Zebulun to fight with—the only tribes willing to join the battle! Who were they against iron chariots?

Nope. He would not go and lead the fight, Barak told her. Not unless she went with him.

Fortunately, the Spirit of God had already given Deborah both foreknowledge of the military outcome and courage to march toward the trouble with Israel's troops. She responded to Barak's hesitancy with a prophecy about the victory: "'Certainly I will go with you,' said Deborah. 'But because of the course you are taking, the honor will not be yours, for the LORD will deliver Sisera into the hands of a woman.' So Deborah went with Barak to Kadesh." (Judges 4:9).

You and I may never be called to face archers and iron chariots like Deborah. We may not be called to run toward the heat of danger. However, because we are God's servants, we may sometimes be called to lead during troubling times and in ways completely unfamiliar to us. American evangelist and freedom fighter Sojourner Truth comes to my mind as a more modern-day example of this kind of call to servant leadership.

Truth's Triumph

Before she escaped to freedom in 1827, Sojourner Truth had

suffered slavery's cruelest effects, having been sold four times and separated from most of her children. Nevertheless, once free, she answered the call to share the gospel message, working for a local minister in the 1830s and becoming a Methodist evangelist in New York in the 1840s. Later, she became the first African American woman to win in a court case against a white slaveholder to regain her young son, who had been sold to a Southern plantation.

A charismatic speaker, Truth also became one of the leading voices in the abolitionist and women's rights movements, helping segregate streetcars in the North, acquiring supplies for Black soldiers during the Civil War, and working with hundreds of former slaves to acquire land and resettle in the North.[1]

Truth's illustrious list of human rights accomplishments in America serves as an example of the power behind a Spirit-led woman called by God to lead, and willing to answer the call. There are many women leaders like her. Could you be one of them, though you may not recognize it presently? Are you willing to answer God's call?

Recognizing Your Leadership

Like Deborah, you may identify yourself as simply "a mother" in your hometown. Being a mother is a noble, honorable role God has given you, for sure. It's one of my most treasured roles, too. But did you know that when you let God's Holy Spirit fill you and guide your thoughts and actions, you become a "turbo-charged" mother? You become a dynamic servant-leader, called by God to lead, not just your children, but other moms, dads, wives, husbands, and single people as well. God made Mother Deborah the judge of thousands of her fellow citizens!

Through the Spirit, other women and men can grow inspired to follow your example of faith, trust God, and live closer to Him because of it. The godly choices you make today as "just a mom" will teach others to make the same wise efforts and will have repercussions far into the future. Never underestimate the power of a woman on whom the Spirit of God rests (1 Corinthians 7:16; 1 Peter 3:1-4; Romans 16:3-4).

What if you're working professionally instead of serving solely at home? The same message applies: Leading others through keeping in step with the Spirit is a wonderful way to honor God, at home or on the job. As an example, I had been serving in a public relations technician role (writer) for more than 15 years when opportunities for promotions to specialist and managerial positions within the department fell into my lap. I felt way out of my comfort zone before applying for each promotion, despite having the credentials and experience needed to fulfill the new titles adequately. Leadership opportunities also arose from the spiritual side of my life during this same time. I was asked to speak at two women's day seminars, something I had never done before. Again, I immediately felt nervously inadequate each time I was asked to present.

Fortunately, God blessed me with godly friends and mentors who helped me realize that my focus had been on me and my limitations, instead of on God and His infinite power and purpose in the tasks He was calling me to do. Through His Spirit, I saw that I didn't have to worry about the outcome of my efforts, because: a) I am God's servant in *every* job or task (Colossians 3:23-24); and b) He was directing my steps. As I prepared for each new application or presentation, the Spirit would encourage me to pray to God for wisdom and for the will to carry out what He desired. And each time I obeyed and surrendered to the Spirit's leading despite my fears, He gave me success in the new role or presentation.

Are you being called by God to some new role of servant-leadership? You may feel intimidated, but don't avoid the call, even if He is calling you to do something you never thought you could undertake, like the call He was about to make to Deborah.

Deborah's Big Reveal

How do you muster the courage to take on a leading role during stressful, challenging moments? I think the courage comes when you know that God's Spirit is with you and when you pray, trust, and rely on Him to direct your steps through the challenges, instead of relying on your own strength, talent, or wisdom to overcome them (Proverbs

3:5-6). It is then that the Spirit does His best work with you and for you, because your heart is malleable and your mind is alert to His directives through the Word of truth.

So it was with Deborah. In Judges 4, the Word tells us she accompanied Barak up to Mount Tabor where the battle was to take place, accompanied by 10,000 Israelite soldiers. Sisera the commander marched out to meet Israel with his iron chariots, but his heavy military equipment became no match for the banks of the Kishon River, situated near the mountain. God had sent a rainstorm and turned the ground around the mountain muddy right as Sisera's chariots approached (Judges 5:20-21). They were stuck and became easy pickings for the Israelites.

Let Deborah's story teach you that, when God decides to use you in His service as a leader, you need not fear answering the call, but answer it praising Him, for He is with you and can be trusted to bring you to success (Judges 5:2; Isaiah 41:10). What an awesome God we serve.

The Spirit Equips You for Service

1. *Fortunately, the Spirit of God had already given Deborah both foreknowledge of the military outcome and courage to march toward the trouble with Israel's troops.*

A. Wisdom, discernment, foreknowledge, courage: Deborah received the proper tools she needed to meet her challenging task. So did Sojourner Truth. What tools do you need to face yours? (See 2 Peter 1:5-7 for a great selection.)

B. As 1 Corinthians 12:4-5 teaches us, "There are different kinds of gifts, but the same Spirit distributes them. There are different kinds of service, but the same Lord." Looking at your gifts, what service do you think God is equipping you to perform among His people? (Read verses 6-11 and see Ephesians 4:11-13 for service examples.)

C. Read Ephesians 6:10-20. As it was for Deborah, it may seem that humans are opposing your life path, but they are not. What pieces of the full armor of God must you still put on to adequately stand against your real foe?

2. God blessed me with godly friends and mentors who helped me realize that my focus had been on me and my limitations, instead of on God and His infinite power and purpose in the tasks He was calling me to do.

A. Read 2 Samuel 12:1-13. Do you have a Nathan in your life?

If so, write a note or send a text to that person right now, letting them know how very grateful you are for their presence in your life.

If not, begin praying now that God would make it clear whom you can ask to be your fine-tuning friend and accountability partner when it comes to helping you live an obedient life to God. Often people will not be that accountability person in your life unless you have asked them, or they know you trust them enough to allow them to do so.

B. Do you think Deborah fulfilled her military service through trusting her past leadership or her ever-present Lord? (See Luke 10:20.)

C. Read the following passages of Scripture and write the words or phrases that indicate in each verse who it is who is strong in the midst of our weaknesses and vulnerabilities:

Psalm 18:

Philippians 4:13:

2 Peter 1:3:

Is it clear to you now that God calls us in our weakness so that He can be strong on our behalf? Don't ever expect you must perform or accomplish on your own. God calls the weak and humble and through them, shows Himself strong.

3. *It is then that the Spirit does His best work with you and for you, because your heart is malleable and your mind is alert to His directives through the Word of truth.*

A. Even Jesus was filled with and guided by the Holy Spirit to accomplish God's will (Matthew 4:1; Luke 4:1). How can you tell when the Spirit is guiding your steps?

B. Read Hebrews 13:20-21. Whom is the Spirit laying on your heart to serve?

C. God gives grace to the humble (James 4:6 KJV); the Holy Spirit is the Spirit of grace (Hebrews 10:29) and truth (John 16:13). How do you know you have been given the Spirit to live in you and guide you in service to God?

14

TAKE CARE OF THE CARETAKER
BY GRACE DARLING

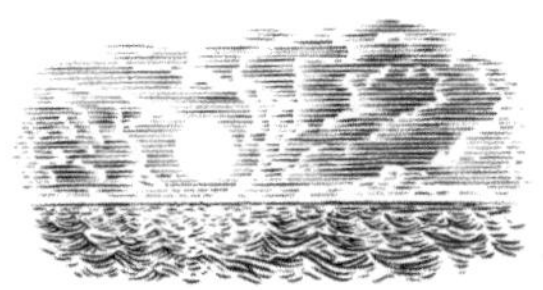

Then, because so many people were coming and going that they did not even have a chance to eat, he said to them, "Come with me by yourselves to a quiet place and get some rest."
MARK 6:31

As a teenager, I prayed to God that I could someday provide for my parents like they had provided for me. Fast forward 40 years. Not only had I lost hope I could ever make that happen, but I had become so physically, mentally, and emotionally exhausted, I could barely breathe.

Inspired by My Parents

Growing up in a family with seven children, I was number six in the bunch. If we were poor, we didn't know much about it because our parents raised us to value people, not material things. Sure, we couldn't afford some things other kids had, but we were clothed and fed and, most of all, we were loved abundantly. My dad, William, showed me the importance of working for a living and providing for one's family by how he provided for us, and I thank God for that (1 Timothy 5:8). But it was my mom, Ida, who trained me in how a matriarch should love and care for her family.

Watching my mom struggle, dedicate, and sacrifice herself for her family gave me great vision and promise that a God-fearing, blessed woman can withstand the pressures of life—and come out looking fabulous. And I mean *fabulous*. I never remember a time when my mother went out of the house looking a mess, or as I like to say it, looking "crazy by the head!" She always carried herself like a lady when she went out. Her hair was together, her clothes matched, and her shoes accented what she wore. Even her attitude was in check. She was simply my inspiration and model for how a lady should carry herself (Proverbs 31). To this day, well into her 80s, she still refuses to go out of the house looking a mess, and so do I.

So, naturally, blessed with such parents, I wanted with all my heart to bless their lives in return. In fact, from my youth into my adult years, I carried one thought, wish, and hope with me—to be able to care for my parents in a monetary way. Yet my income never seemed to allow it. Over the years, I would see my siblings buy my folks things I couldn't afford, and it filled me with longing and sadness that I couldn't give them the same.

Enlightened by the Spirit

But I see now that the Holy Spirit has been hovering over all my decades of longing, sadness, and need. Over the past few years, He has been revealing matters to me about my life that are changing my outlook and restoring my joy.

First, my siblings began teaching me that I had been fulfilling my one dream, hope, and wish all along. You see, since I live closest to our parents' house, I am the child who has always come over to care for their immediate, daily needs as they've aged: house cleaning, lawn care, meal prep, transportation, errands, healthcare assistance. My siblings showed me that, if I added up the value of all these services, I would see that I had been saving my parents a *lot* of money over many years by helping them. I had to learn that giving doesn't stop or start with money, and we can never out-give God (2 Corinthians 9:8). Look at the sacrifice He made: *His Son* (John 3:16). Christ's death was a hard thing for our Father God in heaven to see and endure. But He still gave all He had for you and me.

Because of these conversations with my siblings, I began placing greater value on how I was providing for my parents. I started realizing how Jesus could be pleased that I, like the poor widow, was giving all I had by serving them, giving out of my poverty (Luke 21:3-4). And whenever I started reflecting on my problems, cares, and troubles I would ask myself, *Would you want to switch places with Jesus, or can you endure these few trials you have down here on Earth?* (2 Corinthians 4:17; Colossians 2:14). These days, this question will help me snap out of troubling myself over the cares of the world, and I go on about my prayerful day with laughter and appreciation, with thankfulness in my heart to God.

My Self-Care Crisis

Second, the Spirit helped me realize the pressure that I and, I'm sure, many others put on ourselves as we care for our loved ones. As we love and care for our family members, it is vitally important that we care for ourselves. This is where I went wrong, and it nearly broke me.

Although I loved every moment I spent caring for family and friends in need, I rarely took time for myself or remembered to care for myself. I should have set time aside to give myself some attention (Leviticus 18:18)—to treat myself, to take a day or two away, pamper myself on occasion, or do things I like to do to feel relaxed and at peace with myself.

After nearly two decades of caring for others without performing self-care, I began to wear out. Then, I started losing some of the dearest and closest confidants in my world, within months of each other: my best friend, my sweet older brother, and my favorite uncle. Soon after, my dad's health also started failing; before he passed away, my mom and I did the best we could to help keep him comfortable at home. Just a few months later, a close aunt also died, leaving me to handle some of her affairs. Because I had not cared for myself during those years, tension and stress had built up, and pains and aches had formed in my body.

The month after my aunt died, my mind reached a boiling point.

Out of the blue one morning, I called my two sisters, and I started crying and going on with each one about this and that. I can't even remember the whole conversation. I assume I was at the point of exploding. I thank God that He intervened in my life through my sisters. Recognizing I was at breakpoint, they got together behind the scenes, discussed my condition, and went to work helping me.

They arranged for me to get away for a couple of days to a nice hotel just by myself and even had a masseuse come to the room and give me a full massage. They saw I needed what Jesus prescribed for His disciples: "Come away by yourselves to a secluded place and rest a little while" (Mark 6:31 NLT). It was so wonderful. I was able to regain composure and just think about myself. I'm so grateful they did that for me, because I don't know what could have come about if I did not get that intervention.

Let the Spirit Bring You Balance

Since then, I've come to realize that we must not only take care of family and friends but ourselves. If we don't, we won't be able to care for, love, and help them in the best way, for as long as we'd like to. (It's no surprise that caretakers sometimes pass away earlier than the loved ones they're caring for.) So now, I make sure that every day, at some time during the day, I have a *me* time, whether I'm just sitting at home relaxing to some music and not caring about anything, or reading the Bible, or listening to a sermon. I take time to be at peace with myself daily, whether going for a drive and looking at scenery, or going someplace else I like to visit.

It's an issue of balance to care for others as well as for yourself. If you direct *all* your love and care toward your family, you get off balance; that's where all the pain comes in and the stress, worries, and unhealthy attitudes develop. We need to care for the one and only body that God has blessed us with. We only have one of these; we can't go in the closet and change this body like we can change our clothes and our shoes and even our wigs. No, you only have one body, so make sure you take care of it and give it the love and attention it needs.

May God's Holy Spirit guide you toward proper self-care while you care for your loved ones, and may He give you rest as He gave the Israelites (Isaiah 633:11-14).

The Spirit Gives Rest

1. *Whenever I started reflecting on my problems, cares, and troubles I would ask myself, Would you want to switch places with Jesus, or can you endure these few trials you have down here on Earth?*

A. How do your current trials and sufferings compare to the ones Jesus Christ endured to save you?

B. When discomforting troubles begin flooding your mind, like Grace's did, what scriptures would bring your heart rest instead? Find them, write them on a 3x5 card, and carry the card in your wallet, purse, or pocket, or place the card within reach at your workstation. The Spirit comforts you by reminding you of God's Word (John 14:16-17, 26).

C. Another (and, I think, the best) way to find emotional rest from problems, cares, and troubles is to lay them all on Jesus and leave them with Him to work out for you. Read Matthew 11:28-30 and 1 Peter 5:7. Why would laying your cares on Jesus bring you relief?

2. *They saw I needed what Jesus prescribed for His disciples: "Come away by yourselves to a secluded place and rest a little while" (Mark 6:31 NLT).*

A. Everyone can use secluded rest now and then. Where do you go to find it?

B. When He lived on earth, Jesus "offered up prayers and petitions with fervent cries and tears," asking God to save Him from death (Hebrews 5:7). Do you think He was alone or with others when these times occurred?

C. Name other benefits you gain from resting in seclusion (for example: greater clarity, better sleep, and so on).

3. *We need to care for the one and only body that God has blessed us with.*

A. Bodily rest can come in many forms: physical rest, sensory rest, mental rest, emotional rest, social rest, and creative rest. Which rest could you use the most right now and how will you get it?

B. First Corinthians 6:19-20 teaches that your body is the very temple of God's Holy Spirit, who lives in you. How does rest honor the Spirit?

C. Proper nourishment and rest are two ways we can care for our God-given frame. How else should you care for your body?

PART VII

TEACHING YOU – THE STUDENT

A student is ultimately a discoverer, a learner. When you think of yourself in the student role, I'm guessing you most often picture yourself hitting the books in school. But in reality, the subject matter you and I need to discover most is ourselves.

Troubling times (and how we navigate them) often provide opportunities for self-discovery. They show us areas where we need to grow in our walk with God and help us become more patient (James 1:2-4). Let school social worker Yolanda O'Connor show you how the Holy Spirit can turn life difficulties that surround you into reflective, teachable moments for personal growth.

Of course, the traditional path of the student role involves learning from instructors and books as you work toward a diploma or degree. Oh, the traps, trials, and troubles that can lie within this road of discovery! Still, the Spirit hovers here, even in the midst of those troubles. Walk with me as I share how intimately the Holy Spirit directed my path toward academic and career achievement, despite prior pangs of failure.

15

BE STILL AND KNOW
BY YOLANDA O'CONNOR

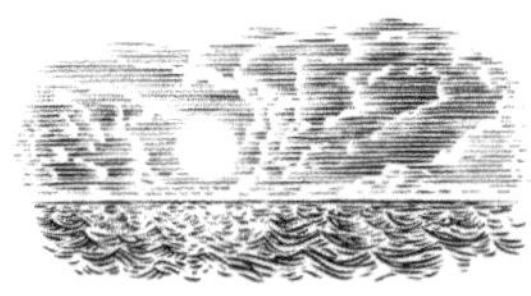

Be still and know that I am God.
PSALM 46:10

Be still and know that I am God." This phrase, from Psalm 46:10, is such a simple yet complicated one, worthy of dissection and honor. While lovely in its simplicity, it is complicated as a command. Why? The idea of being still can be different for each individual.

Why I Did Not Like to Be Still

I have never liked being still. It seemed unfulfilling and just another word for lazy. Why be still when there is still so much to do? I would look with disdain at others who had seemingly mastered this art. I didn't understand how someone could just rest. I didn't understand how someone could just stop and be single-minded in action and task.

But as I have grown older, being still has meant more than having a single-minded focus. It has meant having to look at myself and ask why I do not like to be still. And the answers are both challenging me and changing me.

Trying to Fix Mine and Others' Shortcomings

It seems that whenever I am still, I see the imperfections and shortcomings I possess. Being still also has meant seeing the shortcomings of people I love and being engulfed with inner sadness and despair because I couldn't change them. I knew I wasn't perfect, but surely *I* could help them.

I *used* to think I could help them, often, until one day, the Spirit reminded me through a good friend that I don't have the power to change anyone. This power belongs to God alone (Ezekiel 36:26-27; John 15:5). As I studied the Scriptures further about this, it became clear that being still—for me—meant to make a conscious decision to give up the control that I thought I had.

You see, for me, it has been hard to be still and watch others whom I love live in constant struggle. I had started to develop what I call "survivor's guilt." Because of my guilt, I would try to be the one to change them and their situation. I was definitely not being still and not relying on God to supply the change.

Learning to Embrace the Stillness

These days, however, God's Spirit is teaching me more and more that being still can only happen when I allow myself to know God. I will only know God when I am in His Word and praying. Being *still* has come to mean the *action* of reliance on God and not on myself.

"Be still and know that I am God." When I truly know that He is God, and I am not, I can learn to accept this idea of being still. For when I am still, I can better understand that *He* is moving.

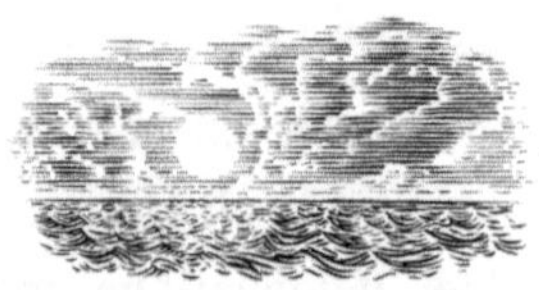

The Spirit Encourages Self-Discovery

1. *The idea of being still can be different for each individual.*

A. What does "being still" mean to you?

B. Read Exodus 14:13-14 and Psalm 27:14. If stressing out about a tough situation cannot deliver you from it, how should you respond to the situation instead?

C. Like Yolanda, you might try to replace body or spirit stillness with busyness or worry. What are some other distractions or replacements for stillness?

2. *It seems that whenever I am still, I see the imperfections and shortcomings I possess.*

A. Read Psalm 4:4. How can stillness be a tool for growth?

B. Why might you not want to see your imperfections and shortcomings?

C. Over the noise of busyness or anxiety, it will be difficult for you to hear the "still, small voice" of God's Holy Spirit providing guidance and wisdom (1 Kings 19:11-13 KJV). What are some ways you can quiet your soul during troubling times?

3. *God's Spirit is teaching me more and more that being still can only happen when I allow myself to know God.*

A. What steps does Yolanda take to know God better?

B. Why would truly knowing God (His nature, abilities, feats, and promises) lead to you to quiet your heart during troubling times?

C. "Allow" yourself to know God; the Spirit will not force your acquaintance with the Father (Proverbs 8:17; Matthew 6:33; Hebrews 11:6).

16

Ruthie: On God's Timing

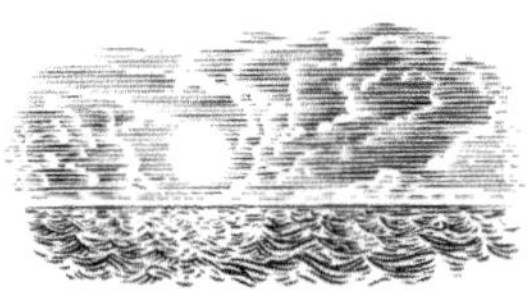

Let us not become weary in doing good,
for at the proper time we will reap a harvest if we do not give up.
GALATIANS 6:9

At first, what gripped me most was fear, a sense of defeat, and complete sadness.

Despite two years of achieving above average grades in all the required courses, I froze while taking the final test—the verbal translation exam—to complete my master's degree in French. *Twice.* I was completely frozen with anxiety and unable to speak *both times*. And since I had only two chances to take the exam, I ended up with absolutely nothing to show for all my hard work.

Now, for someone who had always prided herself on scholastic achievements, this was quite the crushing blow. But what made this heart-crunching failure in my academic career feel even worse was that I knew it was my own fault that it happened. I had been warned it could.

Administrator Advice Unheeded

Two years prior to this exam failure, I was wrapping up my years as an undergrad at Butler University. During the last week of school, my professor, the French department chair at the time, warned me that despite my excellent grades, I wasn't fluent enough in the language to earn a master's degree. (She should know; she was French.) However, having no money to study abroad, no desire to advance my journalism degree (I was a dual major), and no other prospects besides a probationary graduate fellowship in French at the University of Illinois at Urbana-Champaign, I had chosen to take a chance at the master's anyway. It had been a scary, confusing fork in the road for me at that time, and with no career counselors supporting me, I could see no better option than to make what had obviously been the wrong choice.

Or, rather, it was a choice I *thought* had been the wrong one during that moment of graduate-degree defeat and self-doubt. For you see, whether moving past academic failure, advancing professionally, or learning to embrace my life as a single woman, I have discovered one important fact. I have had to wait on God's timing.

Peace and Usefulness During the Wait

When I say "wait," I don't mean just a year or two. Or seven or eight. I mean *wait*, as in Joseph-enslaved-in-Egypt-style waiting[1]. It took me 23 years before reaching again for a master's degree. More than 15 years before earning a job promotion at the office. A decade between longing to marry and marrying.

But the nifty thing is that, as He was with Joseph, the Holy Spirit has been with me in the failure, the longing, and the waiting, bringing me peace and making me useful *during* the wait. The Bible tells us God was with Joseph from the time Joseph was taken captive in Egypt—the very beginning of his life trials (Genesis 39:2, 23). As Joseph waited, God made him useful, both in Potiphar's house and in the dungeon, and God continued to be with him until He elevated Joseph to second-in-command to the most powerful ruler of his day. And, just as Pharaoh recognized that God's Spirit was with Joseph (Genesis 41:38), so I have recognized the Spirit hovering over my waiting, encouraging me to pray and offering peace and guidance, though not at first.

No, not at first. When I realized I had failed that French master's degree for good, I felt like a lonely, rudderless ship. *What do I do*

146

now? I thought. The Spirit encouraged me to wipe my tears, pray, and look for work. I worked part-time proofreading science textbook drafts (and nodding off from it) before landing a job as a cub reporter for a local newspaper. Funny thing is, I don't remember ever having applied for that job; the editor just called me out of the blue and asked when I could start!

I worked less than two years for the paper, but the experience I gained there marked the beginning of my career as a professional writer, editor, and teacher. After leaving the newspaper, I worked as an elementary school teacher's aide, first for visually impaired students and later for academically challenged students. It was during this time I also started dating Brian, whom I married the following year. (Brian would himself become visually impaired a decade later. God works in fascinating ways.)

Five years later, with my husband's gentle encouragement, I moved back into the communication field, as a part-time public relations writer. I first worked for a Champaign clinic and later for Parkland College. Between these gigs, I even had a five-year stretch as a freelance editor for the university while I raised our young family at home (yep, the same school where I had failed to earn my degree).

As I performed nearly two decades of this writing work, I periodically longed for a master's degree. Then one day, God showed up to tell me it was time to pursue one again. And the way He told me was so special, it would be rude for me to deny it was His call.

Administrator Advice Heeded

It was August 2012, with only two weeks remaining before fall semester classes would start. Parkland's Fine and Applied Arts department chair at the time, for whom I had written a major departmental brochure a few months earlier, showed up at my office door. She told me her Basic News Writing instructor had just quit to pursue a job at a national magazine in Chicago. Would I be willing to step in and co-teach her class?

Flattered, I replied, "Well, yes, but I don't have a master's degree."

"Yeah, about that," she said, pushing across my desk a sheet of paper she had brought along with her. It was an information sheet describing the master's degree program in marketing and communication at Franklin University, the very online program I had been noticing for two years but had hesitated to pursue. I would co-teach with a professor for the first year, she explained, but if I wanted to continue teaching the class next year, I must begin earning my master's degree. "Oh, and by the way," she continued, "you can apply annually for professional development funds to help pay for your classes, and Franklin offers tuition reductions to any Parkland employee earning a graduate degree from them."

Did you catch the Spirit hovering over me, watching as God sent one faculty chair to warn me to *wait* on one advanced degree, and another chair (23 years later) to encourage me to *stop waiting* and go after another one? (Such a God move.)

Peace and Usefulness During the Work

As He did for Joseph, God made me useful over the next two years, which included *simultaneous* full-time writer work, part-time instructor work (which helped pay for my remaining tuition expenses), and part-time graduate studies, all on top of supporting my family as a wife, homemaker, and mother of teens! And what I had asked God for at the beginning and throughout that impossible schedule, He gave me—perfect peace in the hustle, as I kept my heart rested on Him (Isaiah 26:3). God also brought me comfort and support through family and friends. For with God, nothing will be impossible (Luke 1:37).

And as it must have been for Joseph, mine has been quite the heady, gratifying reveal.

My Big Reveal

Not only did I earn my Franklin University master's degree in 2015 at age 50, but I was asked to give the graduate student address at our commencement exercises. Next, God used the degree to promote me at my job. *Twice.* (Remember that number?) Within just four years of earning my long-awaited degree, God elevated me from an entry-level writer to second-in-command of the college's marketing department. (Second-in-command—does that sound familiar too?)

What's more, what felt like a life defeat in my eyes (failing to get my first graduate degree) worked out for the good after all, as God has promised to those who love Him (Romans 8:28). Because I had taken all those advanced French classes, I was able to translate a sermon for a French-speaking visitor at the congregation I attended at the time. Years later, I helped some French-speaking students at Parkland navigate to the correct offices they needed. Most recently, my daughter, who also studied French, treated me to an unforgettable week in Paris, where I found I still remembered the language—how to greet people, order food, ask directions, and so on. God never allowed even my degree "failure" to go to waste!

Why We Wait, and What Truly Matters

What about you? How is God teaching you to wait on Him to bring about good for you, even after failure? Are you patiently making yourself useful inside the waiting and praising God even if your change might not come? Or is your heavenly Father simply not working things out fast enough for you, and you're just tired of Abraham-, Moses-, or Joseph-style waiting? Are you running ahead of Him, trying to manipulate your outcome in ways He wouldn't approve? Oh, I've been there, too, and I can still be there at times; yet, somehow, my impatience never seems to produce the desired results. (Big surprise.) I thank God for His patience with me, for I am truly a work in progress in this area.

God knows you and I get weary of waiting for Him to resolve our problems. But His timing is still everything. You can trust His timing and wait on it. Let Psalm 27:14 and Isaiah 40:31 teach you that your waiting is not an exercise in futility. During this time, God is working to strengthen and renew your heart. King David recognized that it was God's Holy Spirit who would renew his own compromised spirit toward God (Psalm 51:10). And while you wait and trust, study. Studying and meditating on God's Word as a life practice allows the Spirit to renew your mind so that you walk more closely within the will of God during times of trouble and waiting (Romans 12:2).

Through my time of waiting on Him, God showed me what matters most in this life is not the successes or failures, or even the blessings or sufferings. No, what matters most is believing He is real and is within me, takes care of me, and has plans for me here and in eternity (Hebrews 11:6; Jeremiah 29:11). What matters most is remaining in His will and in His love through mindful adherence to His Word. What He told Paul, He is telling me: No matter what I'm waiting for—be it rescue or blessing—I must trust Him by patiently bringing Him honor and glory *within* the waiting, for His favor is all I need (2 Corinthians 12:9). He's telling you the same.

Amen, Lord! I will do my best to wait for You. For I believe that You, Yahweh, my Mighty God, have a marvelous future in store for me and for all those who love Your Son and show that love by obediently following Your commands.

Now that will be the *real* big reveal for you and me, one so worth waiting for.

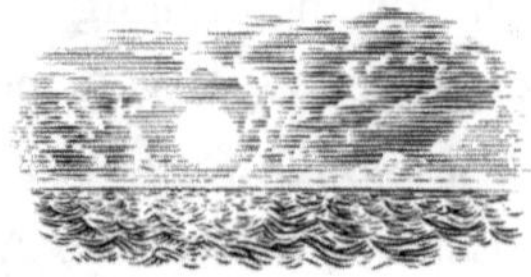

The Spirit Blesses Your Waiting

1. *When I realized I had failed that French master's degree for good, I felt like a lonely, rudderless ship.*

A. How do you move past the disappointment of what seems like a major life "failure?"

B. Read 2 Corinthians 12:9. What insight does it give you on the purpose of failure?

C. I may have felt rudderless, but was I? (See Romans 8:28.)

Who was really steering my life's course?

2. As *He was with Joseph, the Holy Spirit has been with me in the failure, the longing, and the waiting, bringing me peace and making me useful during the wait.*

A. Read Genesis 39, especially verses 2-5 and 21-23. Being a prisoner can seem like a major life failure, but God has a useful purpose for you even through such a trial. What was His purpose for Joseph?

B. Joseph waited approximately 13 years between his enslavement in Egypt and becoming that nation's vice-regent. What do his words and actions indicate about his attitude during this time?

C. Read Philippians 5:7 (preferably in the KJV for this question). When have you seen God's Holy Spirit bring you "peace that passes all understanding" during a difficult waiting period?

Take a moment and thank Him for being with you through that troubling time.

3. *Through my time of waiting on Him, God showed me that what matters most in this life is not the successes or failures in it, or even the blessings or sufferings in it.*

A. Since the days of Adam and Eve, God has only wanted us to see and understand that we are blessed when we rely on His loving care for us and walk solely in His purpose for us (Genesis 1:27-29, 2:8-9; Jeremiah 29:11). How are you doing when it comes to relying on what matters most?

B. Why should you not worry when life brings you failure, disappointment, or suffering? (See Isaiah 43:1-7 for a hint.)

C. God is still teaching you what matters most when you wait on Him to provide. What is His Spirit walking you through today?

PARTING THOUGHTS AND VIPS

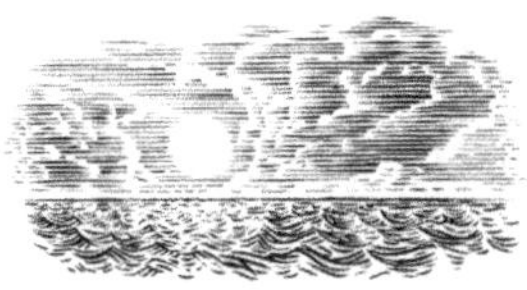

But thou art holy, O thou that inhabitest the praises of Israel.
Our fathers trusted in thee: they trusted, and thou didst deliver them.
They cried unto thee, and were delivered: they trusted in thee,
and were not confounded.

PSALM 2:3-5 KJV

I love something I once read about our hovering Holy Spirit: "When you begin a relationship with God, the Holy Spirit comes into your life. He is with you through the good and the bad. You can choose to ignore the Holy Spirit's influence, but He will never leave you. He is always waiting for you to turn back and seek His comfort, wisdom and guidance.

The Holy Spirit can help you experience and have a deeper understanding of God's love for you. His presence in your life means you are never on your own."[1]

Just like these godly women from the Scriptures and from present-day life, you and I have a choice in how to respond to the trials, troubles, and challenges that weave in and out of our lives. We can choose either to *react* to them, or to *act* on them. (And while *inaction* may seem to be a third option, it functions as one of the two prior choices, depending on the situation.) The former choice, *reaction*, relies on the flesh; the latter choice, *action*, relies on the Spirit. It serves us best to take the following *action* steps whenever we face new difficulties or challenges, no matter the size:

1. Pause before responding.
2. Call on the Spirit's leading.
3. Look for His answer.

Pause. Call. Look. We'll unwrap these steps in a moment.

Letting the Spirit in to Encourage You

Are you feeling discouraged about a loved one's death, clashes with your spouse, a mean boss, chronic suffering, sin, failure, loneliness, guilt, mounting debt, backbiting comments, or some other situation? Can that discouragement sometimes tempt you to think you've been defeated? I can relate. I have felt that way too. But take heart. As long as we're still alive, there's hope for guidance through the challenges. Christ has overcome the world and all its discouragement (John 16:33), and He left His Spirit with us so we can overcome it, too.

Whatever troubling times you're experiencing right now, whatever your murky, dark, formless void, the Holy Spirit has the right path for you to take to overcome the trouble. He can get you on the path that leads from discouragement to joy. And it all starts with letting Him in. Sure, He's hovering over you even now, waiting, watching, and encouraging prayer as God transforms and matures you. But as an active, engaging Spirit, He is also ready to step in and give you comfort and guidance along the path, when you let Him.

As part of the Godhead, the Holy Spirit longs to be actively involved as you try to navigate the murky waters of life. God made you, Christ saved you, and the Spirit seeks to walk with you, side by side, guiding your steps in righteous actions until Christ's return. After all, it's the Spirit's turn to shine God's love on you (John 14:16-17).

Be aware, though, of a very important point (VIP #1): It grieves the Holy Spirit whenever we ignore His nudges, refuse to follow His godly truth-whispers, or keep Him at a distance instead of keeping in step with Him (Ephesians 4:30; Galatians 5:16-26). Has the Spirit said something to your heart for you to do, or to stop doing, to honor God? (Yes, He literally *speaks* to us and for us; see John 16:13 and Romans 8:26.) Has He led you to some life challenge and left you wondering about the next steps? Good. Now that you're aware of it, ask yourself: *Am I following His lead or ignoring His guidance? Am I tackling the challenge by myself or trustingly and attentively leaning in to Him for divine wisdom?*

Too often, I've chosen to ignore the Spirit's promptings and face troubles in my own strength. Whenever I do, I discover the choice to be a big mistake, but sometimes not soon enough for the damage to be undone. Yes, these are questions every child of God would do well to ask themselves regularly. As John Piper aptly put it, "The Holy Spirit lives in us to help us, if we will yield ourselves to His leading. When we rest in the salvation that Jesus provided and rely on the Holy Spirit to help us navigate the dangerous world around us, we can keep from being troubled in our hearts."[2]

So, how can we know we're letting the Spirit in and keeping in step with Him? How can we ensure we are acting on, not reacting to, life's trials as they unfold? Let's look at those earlier *action* steps more closely: Pause. Call. Look. I believe we'll find that the best answers lie within those steps.

Action Steps Explained

1. ***Pause before responding.*** You will gain the strength to handle whatever trial or challenge you're facing when you pause before reacting and do a sort of check-in with Jesus first (Isaiah 40:31). Sometimes, it only takes a moment: a quick, close-eyed prayer for wisdom and guidance (or an open-eyed one. See Nehemiah 2:1-5), or just a minute or two to examine your situation in light of the One who sees you and can fix anything and everything.

For example, before lashing out from hurt, anger, or frustration at something family members have said or done, I have been known to rise from wherever I'm sitting, head straight for the bathroom, and close the door to pray (Matthew 6:6). In there, I briefly lay out my complaint to God and *beg* Him for a more loving, patient attitude than the one I'm experiencing at the moment, one more in keeping with His will for me. (In fact, Brian and the kids had become so familiar with this practice over the years, they sometimes mistook my legitimate bathroom breaks for quick-prayer check-ins!) And after every pause—thank the good Lord—He has delivered. He has never once failed to upgrade my heart with greater peace by the time I exited the (water) closet. After all, He wants me to cast every care on His shoulders, no matter how small, and to seek His wisdom for life at every turn (1 Peter 5:7).

Alternatively, whenever I haven't paused before reacting, I have walked myself (and walked by myself) into confusion, anger, pride, and misjudgment. Failure. Whenever I have ignored the Spirit's guidance, refused to seek it, or been too busy defending, avenging, or comforting myself even to notice it, I have grieved God's Holy Spirit, stunted my growth, and blocked my strength renewal. And oh, how I have grieved Him so many times through the years in big and small ways, those times He was clearly showing me that another way was the better, godlier path to take but I chose to do things my way (the way of the flesh) instead. Just one trusting pause to seek the Spirit's will and obey His voice before reacting could have saved me from days, weeks, and even years of repercussions. Again, I'm so glad we have forgiveness in our patient Lord.

2. *Call on the Spirit's leading.* The reason for pausing before (re)action is not to seek your own understanding of how to handle your challenge or trial, nor to seek another person's opinion about it. Calling on wisdom from any other source than what God gives through His Spirit is folly and yields unsatisfactory results (Proverbs 3:5-6; Psalm 118:8-9). Since God's way is perfect, His holy Word (the sword of the Spirit[3]) will provide you with the perfect answers for the perplexities you face[4].

Now, this is not to say there is little benefit in godly counsel. To the contrary, God often uses His children to offer the "excellent oil" of corrective counsel to one another (Psalm 141:5). But this counsel has its roots in Jesus Christ—the Way, the Truth, and the Life—and not in any human wisdom. Even here, though, be wary like an excellent Berean![5] Study Christ's teaching for yourself, so you can discern whether the counsel you're receiving is truly from the Spirit of Christ. People sometimes twist or distort Jesus' teachings to suit selfish motives (2 Peter 3:16). If we accept what seems like their godly counsel without hiding God's Word in our hearts, we could be led aside from the Spirit's true path for us (Psalm 1:1-2; 119:11).

Yes, God's hovering Holy Spirit will guide you through the murky waters, the deep, rushing rivers, and the red-hot, flaming valleys of life.

He is there for you and is with you, so call out for His wisdom. And again, if you're not in the strict training of studying Jesus' teaching (1 Corinthians 9:25), it's time to start, so you can discern whether any direction you receive in your mind or through godly people is truly from Christ. But don't stop there.

3. *Look for His answer.* The Spirit wants to bring to your memory the Word (which is Christ[6]) at the times you need it most. (John 14:26). I think we often fail to realize this very important point (VIP #2). A good practice is to take 5-10 minutes in a quiet place (for me, it's usually in bed at night) to just *listen* for a word from the Spirit. If a rambling thought tries to come into your mind instead, just let it flow out as easily as it came in and keep on listening to your breath or the soft beat of your heart. God sometimes has an insight waiting there in the quiet place, one just for you. That insight can realign you with His will, center you in His love, or provide a prompting toward action. And this insight will likely come to you, not like a rushing wind, rumbling earthquake, or blazing fire, but like a soft, gentle whisper (1 Kings 19:11-13). Quiet insights like these have been transformative in my life.

My last very important point (VIP #3) for you is, I believe, the most comforting of them all. The Holy Spirit that hovers over you at this very moment will not leave you but will be with you *forever* (John 14:16). If you allow Him, He will be waiting, watching, encouraging prayer, comforting, and guiding you in the Word of Truth until your final big reveal. Do you know what your *final* big reveal will look like? Perhaps you don't fully know, but Christ has given you some hints. You will...

> ...be like Jesus (2 Corinthians 3:18 BSB)
> ...know all things (1 Corinthians 13:12)
> ...be able to see Jesus as He is (1 John 3:2)
> ...fly (1 Thessalonians 4:17)
> ...wear royal clothing (Revelation 7:9)
> ...be weepy—in a good way (Revelation 7:17)
> ...never die (John 11:26 KJV)

...be like angels (Luke 20:36)

...have no pain, toil, or troubles (Revelation 21:4)

...be eternally happy (Matthew 25:23)

Now, even with all you still don't yet know about it, isn't *that* big reveal worth whatever troubles you're facing right in this moment?

UNWRAP THE GIFT OF THE SPIRIT

Did you know the Holy Spirit is the perfect wedding present? Have you unwrapped this precious gift for your life by accepting Jesus Christ? If you're not quite certain that you have, allow me to explain further how to unwrap the gift.

People whom Jesus saves are collectively called the bride of Christ (Ephesians 5:25-27; Revelation 19:7-9). During a wedding, the bride and groom typically make "I do" or "I will" promises to each other. The would-be spouses state these commitments, or vows, publicly. In some cultures, a family must pay a dowry to a groom to accept a bride; in other cultures, the groom must pay the bride's family to receive her (Genesis 29:18).

Marry Christ, Receive the Gift

Desiring to be your groom, Christ openly has declared His commitment to you through His death on the cross (Ephesians 5:1-2). He has made promises to love you, and He sacrificed Himself to purchase you as His bride. His death on the cross is the ultimate "I do" in the Christian's relationship with Him.

Of course, marriage vows are not a one-sided deal. To become the bride of Jesus Christ, you must make some "I do" decisions as well, decisions that openly profess your desire to become one with Christ and your commitment to living forever with Him.

"I do" believe, confess Christ as Lord, and turn away from sin.

Believe that Jesus Christ is the Son of God and that He died to save you from sin and death—this is the first and most important decision you make toward life as a Christian. Without believing in Christ, you cannot be saved by Him (Hebrews 11:6).

You must make other decisions too. Turning away from the sin in your life and publicly confessing your belief in Christ are two vital decisions toward salvation. Repenting of wrongdoing and rebellion against God and openly acknowledging His Son indicate your trust in Christ's Lordship over your life (Revelation 3:20; Romans 10:9-14). Does making these decisions mean you'll never sin again? No, but it does mean you are now committing yourself to living a life of continued repentance from sin and confession of Christ's Lordship over you.

"I do" choose to be baptized.

Having sincerely and openly believed in Christ and repented of your sins, you must also be baptized (Matthew 18:28). In doing so, Christ removes the guilt of your sins by His blood. It is in baptism (covering by water and blood) that you finally clothe yourself with Christ, coming up out of the water as a new creation with no more stain of sin. You have now been born again and given the Holy Spirit of God (John 3:5). And Christ's blood continues to cleanse you whenever you sin in the future (1 John 1:7-10).

Other verses linking baptism with our salvation include:

- Acts 2:38-41 "And Peter said to them, 'Repent, and be baptized every one of you in the name of Jesus Christ for the forgiveness of your sins; and you shall receive the gift of the Holy Spirit." (See also Acts 9:17-18).
- John 3:3-5: "Jesus answered, 'Very truly I tell you, no one can enter the kingdom of God unless they are born of water and the Spirit.'
- Mark 16:16: "Whoever believes and is baptized will be saved, but whoever does not believe will be condemned."
- Acts 22:16: "And now why do you wait? Rise and be baptized, and wash away your sins, calling on his name" (See also Acts 9:17-18).
- 1 Peter 3:21 "Baptism ... now saves you ..."
- Acts 8:36-38: "Look, here is water. What can stand in the way of my being baptized?"
- Other important verses about baptism are Romans 6:3-4, 1 Corinthians 6:11, and Titus 3:5.

"I do" choose to stay faithful to Christ.

What good is a vow if you break it? As God is faithful to us in all His promises, so we must be faithful in our commitment to follow Jesus His Son. So train yourself in godliness through studying His Word so that you remain in His righteousness and do not abandon the faith (1 Timothy 4:1-10).

Be sure to neglect none of these important "I do's" as you put on Christ! Unwrap the gift of the Holy Spirit by uniting with the Son!

FOOD FOR THOUGHT

Questions for Small-Group Study

Chapter 1 - Martha: But Even Now

1. In John 11, verses 5-6 and 14-15, we get a sense of Jesus' motivation for delaying in getting to Lazarus. One little word, "So," in verse 5 shows He did it out of love for Lazarus' family, and "for your sake" in verse 15 shows He did it also to help His followers. What other reasons might He delay delivering us from troubles?

2. Have you ever been "refined in the kiln of troublesome times" and come out of it a stronger person? Discuss.

Chapter 2 - When God Calls You by Name

1. "God opens our eyes in His time to reveal Himself to us" is a powerful truth. Tell of a time the Spirit *called your name*, giving you greater recognition of God's presence in your life.

2. Sins like fear, impurity, unforgiveness, and pride build barriers between us and God (Isaiah 59:2) that keep Him from heeding our prayers and prevent us from recognizing His will in our daily decisions and situations. Tell of a time when, like Kendra, you did not recognize that an "internal nudge toward better choices" came from Him.

Chapter 3 - Sarah: Taken by Another Man

1. Sarah showed quiet submission to Abraham's decisions, even when they seemed to go against her best interests or safety. In what area(s) can you imitate this faith-filled submission with your husband?

2. Sarah grew richer in finances and faith each time she trusted in God and followed her husband's requests for secrecy. Take some time to consider, then discuss: How has God rewarded you whenever you have placed your trust in Him?

Chapter 4 - Abigail: Staving Off Disaster

1. What can we glean from Abigail's life with Nabal when our spouses become fussy, anxious, critical, or otherwise less than attractive?

2. God went from potentially destroying Abigail to adding blessings, because she courageously and generously gave to David and his men, with humble gratitude. In the buffet of blessings you gratefully give back to God, which of these items do you withhold more from Him: time, talent, money, energy, or wisdom?

Chapter 5 - Hannah: Giving a Child to God

1. As He did with the Israelites, God expects us to show our gratefulness for fertility by teaching our children about Him and reminding them of His goodness and faithfulness. Is this your singular goal with your child(ren)? If not, what's stopping you from obedience to this command?

2. Dedicating your children to God doesn't ensure that, once they reach the accountability of adulthood, they will stay faithfully obedient to Him. However, they're still your children. In what ways do you continue to dedicate their lives to God? Read Job 1:1-5 as one example of a best practice.

Chapter 6 - Rizpah: Protective Even in Death

1. Even the strongest of Christian women can be tempted to doubt God's love during troubling times. What scriptures do you turn to when such doubts threaten your heart?

2. God waited until after Rizpah's agonized yearning to bury her sons honorably was satisfied before He healed the land from famine. How do you think God's Spirit felt as He watched her weep over their corpses?

3. When have you seen God grant a specific desire of your heart, one you had shared with no one but Him?

Chapter 7 - Ruth: Loss, Loyalty, and Love

1. Read Matthew 5:16. How did Naomi exhibit faith while suffering a tragic loss?

2. How did her example affect her daughter-in-law Ruth?

3. The Spirit specializes in hovering over the difficult, unfamiliar places in our lives, providing strength and encouraging prayer. What similar places have you faced lately?

4. Have you noticed His presence there with you? In what ways?

Chapter 8 - Praise Inside the Pain

1. The Holy Spirit not only encourages us to pray, but to praise God, as we ride on our troubled seas. Why must we praise God in the midst of trouble? (See Psalm 46:1-3 for a hint.)

2. Read Habakkuk 3:17-19 once more. Pam's mother was an inspiring example of faith to her daughter at their moment of greatest grief. What did her mother's actions at her dear husband's deathbed teach Pam about having a relationship with God?

Chapter 9 - Like Mother, Like Daughter

1. If the Spirit hovers over us during physically abusive scenarios like those Plashan suffered, why doesn't He intervene to stop the abuser each time?

2. How else might God be working out such troubling times for our good?

3. Many abused children become child abusers themselves. Discuss how the Spirit worked to prevent Plashan from imitating her mother's style of parenting with her own daughters. What was the outcome?

Chapter 10 - Leah: Starting from Less Than

1. When someone you love leads you to feel "less than," what scriptures can you hide in your heart to feel secure in God's love?

2. Leah moved from seeking adoration from man to giving adoration to God. What do you think were the factors in her life that caused this change of attitude?

Chapter 11 - Zelophehad's Daughters: A United Front

1. The Holy Spirit hovers over us, not just individually, but collectively as well. What did He prompt the sisters to do as a unit?

2. What does He inspire Christ's believers to do as one body?

3. "For good or evil, a plan backed by unity cannot easily be ignored; it must be reckoned with." How has God intervened to support unified actions or decisions you've made with others?

Chapter 12 - Esther: Daring to Confront

1. Sometimes, the Holy Spirit encourages us not only to pray, but to fast as well. Read Ezra 8:23. Have you ever had a yearning to fast while petitioning God?

2. Why might we not fast though prompted in our spirits to do so?

3. Read Job 42:7-9. The Jews prayed for Esther's success and safety in approaching Xerxes. Why is God moved by intercessory prayer?

4. What other biblical examples are there of such petitioning?

Chapter 13 - Deborah: Called to Lead

1. How can you tell the Spirit of God rests on you, as He rested on Deborah?

2. Deborah and Sojourner Truth were "just moms" who answered God's call to new roles of servant-leadership during troubling times. In what new ways have you been called to lead throughout your life?

Chapter 14 - Take Care of the Caretaker

1. Has the Spirit ever shown you that you had already received the blessing you were longing for—or, alternatively, that you were better off not having received what you wanted? Elaborate.

2. The Spirit helped Grace realize "it's an issue of balance to care for others as well as for yourself." Why might we as women have difficulty prioritizing self-care?

Chapter 15 - Be Still and Know

1. The concept of being still can have different meanings for everyone. What first comes to your mind when you hear the words "be still?"

2. Although His thoughts are far higher than ours, God says we can know He is God. What does this mean?

3. What did Yolanda do to know Him better?

4. How much closer are you to knowing God than you were 10 years ago? Assess if your practices are moving you closer to knowing God or if you need to make adjustments.

Chapter 16 - Ruthie: On God's Timing

1. Think of some "Joseph-enslaved-in-Egypt-style waiting" you're experiencing, years with no affirmative answer from God. Why might God be holding back from granting your request?

2. How might this waiting work out for your good?

3. "What matters most in this life is not the successes, failures, blessings, or sufferings; it is believing that God is real, is with you, takes care of you, and has plans for you." Do you believe this? Why?

4. What can you do to bring greater focus to what matters most?

NOTES

Chapter 3 - Sarah: Taken by Another Man

　　1. Judges 19:24; Genesis 19:6-8.

Chapter 4 - Abigail: Staving Off Disaster

　　1. Ecclesiastes 9:1.

Chapter 5 - Hannah: Giving a Child to God

　　1. Mark 10:30.

　　2. Exodus 1:19.

　　3. Ephesians 6:4.

　　4. Ecclesiastes 12:1.

　　5. Luke 16:27-30.

　　6. 1 Samuel 25:1.

Chapter 6 - Rizpah: Protective Even in Death

　　1. Joshua 9:1-27.

　　2. Psalm 51:4.

　　3. 2 Samuel 12: 13-25.

Chapter 7 - Ruth: Loss, Loyalty, and Love

　　1. Genesis 19:37.

　　2. Ruth 4:16-22.

Chapter 9 - Like Mother, Like Daughter

　　1. To find an Adult Children of Alcoholics (ACoA) meeting near you, visit adultchildren.com or your local public health department. The American Psychological Association also offers tips for locating a mental health therapist, at apa.org/ptsd-guideline/patients-and-families/finding-good-therapist.

Chapter 10 - Leah: Starting from Less Than

　　2. Cindi McMenamin, *When Women Walk Alone: Finding Strength Through the Seasons of Life* (Eugene, OR: Harvest House Publishers, 2002), p. 34. For more on Cindi's book, see her website: www.StrengthForTheSoul.com.

Chapter 11 - Zelophehad's Daughters: A United Front

　　1. Mwaniki, Lydia (2018). *"Bible study: The daughters of Zelophehad,"*

from https://learn.tearfund.org/en/resources/footsteps/footsteps-101-110/footsteps-105/bible-study-the-daughters-of-zelophehad, accessed February 16, 2023.

Chapter 12 - Esther: Daring to Confront

1. Esther 4:11; 1:10-19.
2. Esther 2:5-10.
3. Esther 3:1-11.
4. Esther 4:12-14.
5. Esther 4:25-17.
6. Esther 5:1-8.
7. Esther 7:1-2.
8. Esther 2:21-23; 6:1-11.
9. Esther 5:9 14; 7:3-10.
10. Esther 9:1-19.
11. Esther 9:20-32.

Chapter 13 - Deborah: Called to Lead

1. Michal, Debra, ed., *"Biography: Sojourner Truth,"* from https://www.womenshistory.org/education-resources/biographies/sojourner-truth, accessed February 16, 2023.

Chapter 16 - Ruthie: On God's Timing

1. Genesis 37:2; 41:46.

Parting Thoughts and VIPs

1. Eng, Faith. "God's Love Scripture Verses in the Bible," from https://www.cru.org/us/en/train-and-grow/spiritual-growth/gods-love-scriptures.html, accessed February 16, 2023

2. Piper, John (Jan. 4, 2022). "Let Not Your Heart Be Troubled," Got Questions Ministries. Found at https://www.gotquestions.org/let-not-your-heart-be-troubled.html, accessed February 16, 2023

3. Ephesians 6:17.
4. 2 Samuel 22:31.
5. Acts 17:11.
6. John 1:1-14.

About the Author

Ruthie Counter is an experienced Bible teacher who has encouraged and helped women understand and apply the Word for more than 30 years. She provides spiritual mentorship and has been a guest speaker at Christian women's seminars. Ruthie works as a public relations and marketing writer in Illinois. She and her husband Brian have two children, Megan and David. You can connect with her at **www.thespirithovers.com**.

Contributing Writers

Grace Darling has a passion for service. A longtime Christian, Grace has owned a facility cleaning business for many years, servicing both nonprofit organizations and residential clients. Along with offering interior maintenance services, Grace also has provided personal grooming, meal preparation, and lawn care services to family and friends within Indiana, where she resides. She is the proud mother of an adult son and relishes spending time with loved ones.

Dr. Pamela Lau is an Asian American immigrant from the Republic of Singapore. Her first home church was Elim Church in Singapore where she came to know Jesus Christ as her Lord and Savior, served as a youth group leader, and taught Sunday school. While an undergraduate at the University of Singapore, she actively participated in the Varsity Christian Fellowship (VCF); upon graduation, she served as a VCF campus minister for three years. In 1980, Pam came to the United States as an international student. The Lord led her and her husband, Lawson, to become involved with ministry to international students and their families on several college campuses. Pam serves as president of Parkland College, a community college in Illinois, and she continues to support Lawson in ministry as he pastors All Nations Baptist Church.

Kendra McClure is a wife and mom of three from Illinois. She began learning about Jesus at a young age and has identified as a Christian throughout her life, but she didn't truly know Jesus until an encounter with the Spirit while she was undergoing treatments for breast cancer. Now in remission, Kendra has developed a heart for evangelism and complements her career as a college instructor with writing and speaking about walking in faith through cancer.

Dr. Plashan McCune is a Christian, wife, and mother of two amazing young women. Her professional experiences include roles as a juvenile detention officer, foster care case manager, youth development leader, teacher, school counselor, assistant principal, principal, and mental health professional. She currently serves as executive director of Higher Learning U Inc. and CEO of the Black Homeownership Project. Besides her daughters, two things Plashan feels most proud of are leading the African American Young Ladies Summit Program (AAYLS) and authoring the book *Trauma and Postsecondary Success: A Framework for Systemic Change* (2019). She lives in Colorado.

Yolanda O'Connor is a Christian, wife, and mother who co-directs a grant-funded youth services program in Illinois. Concurrently, she is completing her master's degree in social work and aspires to be a motivational speaker. Originally from Chicago, Yolanda's spiritual foundation started in her home as a young child, but her true connection with God came as a freshman at the University of Illinois.